Hekate

The Ultimate Guide to Understanding the Goddess of Witchcraft and Ancient Greek Magic

© Copyright 2023 - All rights reserved.

The content contained within this book may not be reproduced, duplicated, or transmitted without direct written permission from the author or the publisher.

Under no circumstances will any blame or legal responsibility be held against the publisher, or author, for any damages, reparation, or monetary loss due to the information contained within this book, either directly or indirectly.

Legal Notice:

This book is copyright protected. It is only for personal use. You cannot amend, distribute, sell, use, quote or paraphrase any part, or the content within this book, without the consent of the author or publisher.

Disclaimer Notice:

Please note the information contained within this document is for educational and entertainment purposes only. All effort has been executed to present accurate, up-to-date, reliable, and complete information. No warranties of any kind are declared or implied. Readers acknowledge that the author is not engaging in the rendering of legal, financial, medical, or professional advice. The content within this book has been derived from various sources. Please consult a licensed professional before attempting any techniques outlined in this book.

By reading this document, the reader agrees that under no circumstances is the author responsible for any losses, direct or indirect, that are incurred as a result of the use of the information contained within this document, including, but not limited to, errors, omissions, or inaccuracies.

Your Free Gift
(only available for a limited time)

Thanks for getting this book! If you want to learn more about various spirituality topics, then join Mari Silva's community and get a free guided meditation MP3 for awakening your third eye. This guided meditation mp3 is designed to open and strengthen ones third eye so you can experience a higher state of consciousness. Simply visit the link below the image to get started.

https://spiritualityspot.com/meditation

Table of Contents

INTRODUCTION 1
CHAPTER 1: WHO IS HEKATE...REALLY? 3
CHAPTER 2: THE HEKATEAN WITCH 14
CHAPTER 3: HEKATE'S SIGNS AND SYMBOLS 23
CHAPTER 4: CONNECTING WITH HEKATE 34
CHAPTER 5: HEKATEAN HERBLORE 45
CHAPTER 6: CREATING AN ALTAR FOR HEKATE 60
CHAPTER 7: THE DEIPNON AND OTHER RITUALS 69
CHAPTER 8: HEKATEAN SPELLWORK 78
CHAPTER 9: DIVINATION WITH HEKATE 89
BONUS: ORPHIC HYMN TO HEKATE 99
CONCLUSION 101
HERE'S ANOTHER BOOK BY MARI SILVA THAT YOU MIGHT LIKE 103
YOUR FREE GIFT (ONLY AVAILABLE FOR A LIMITED TIME) 104
REFERENCES 105

Introduction

Whether you take an interest in the world of witchcraft or enjoy exploring the legends, mythologies, and stories of Ancient Greece, you've likely heard about the goddess Hekate. She has been a prominent figure in witchcraft for centuries due to her association with the underworld, crossroads, and the triple moon. Her stories feature her as a protector and guide, often portraying her doing magic and casting spells. Hekate, the guardian of the underworld, was believed to practice magic and perform rituals to guide and protect those journeying her territory.

Hekate also taught the goddesses Medea and Circe invaluable divination skills, such as the practice of herbal magic. This is why she is regarded as a symbol of guidance among the practitioners of magic. Wiccans hold Hekate in the highest regard, as they worship her as the deity of magic, darkness, and the moon.

This book serves as the ultimate guide to everything there is to know about Hekate as the goddess of witchcraft and ancient Greek magic. It delves deep into her attributes, mythos, powers, and archetypes and provides insight into how to safely work with her spiritually and ritualistically. Even though the book comprises comprehensive and historical accounts of the goddess, it's quite easy to understand and follow. This guide is suitable for those new to ancient Greek and witchcraft worlds and more seasoned readers alike.

By reading this book, you'll understand who Hekate really is, a multi-faceted deity who means different things to different people, and find out how she's regarded in the modern world. The book also explores the term "Hekatean witch" and helps you determine how drawn you are to the deity and the best way to go about your practice. You'll learn about the various signs, tools, and symbols associated with the goddess and get to know the origins of the "Hekate's Wheel" or the Stropholos. You'll then find a practical exercise encouraging you to draw on your intuitive abilities to create a unique Hekate symbol.

You should be ready to initiate a connection with Hekate after reading the first few chapters, which is why chapter 4 serves as a step-by-step guide on how to make contact with the goddess. You'll find instructions and tips on performing certain meditations and visualizations that will help you access your intuition and a higher state of consciousness. The following chapter delves deep into Hekatean herblore and elaborates on the herbs most commonly associated with the deity.

This book also provides instructions on creating your own altar and adjusting it to appeal to Hekate. You'll find recommendations on which tools to incorporate into your shrine, guidance on consecrating and blessing them, and ideas on how to use them to strengthen your connection with the goddess. You'll understand how to make appropriate offerings and conduct various practical rituals. You'll also learn about the spells you can use to pray to Hekate and everything associated with her. Finally, you'll discover how to incorporate Hekatean magic into divination practices.

Chapter 1: Who Is Hekate...Really?

Hekate or Hecate is a multi-faceted deity who means different things to different people. In ancient times, she was viewed as a three-formed (trimorphos), key-bearing (kleidouchos), and light/torch-bearing (phosphoros) goddess who resides on the roads and crossroads (einodia). She is associated with entranceways, night, light, liminal rites, and transitions.

Hekate, or Hecate, is a multifaced deity in Greek mythology.
https://jenikirbyhistory.getarchive.net/amp/media/hekate-6e0c17

Hekate is one of the most prominent deities in Greek mythology. She is portrayed as a "soteira," or savior of souls because she saved Persephone, the goddess of Spring and the dead after Hades (god of the underworld) kidnaped her. According to the Chaldean Oracles, Hekate is also a world soul. Throughout history, her role has changed, with Medievalists and her worshipers limiting her role to only a goddess of witches and sorcery.

Nowadays, many women idolize her and view her as a feminist icon. However, she is often portrayed as a dark goddess or an entity that one can call upon for favors or vengeance. This is an unfair representation of what this powerful goddess truly represents. She can't be placed under one category since her personality has many different aspects; you'll discover those as you learn more about her.

So, who is Hekate, really? Is she good or evil? Is she a savior or a dark goddess? This chapter will uncover the mystery of Hekate and show you her true identity.

The Name and Titles of Hekate

In Greek transliteration, Hekate is spelled Hekate, derived from the male name Hekatos, a term used to describe the sun god Apollo, meaning "the one who works from afar." However, no one knows the real origin of her name. In fact, some scholars argue that having a Greek name doesn't mean that she originated from ancient Greece, as some trace her roots to Caria in Asia Minor, which is located in modern-day Turkey.

In ancient Rome, Hekate was called Trivia, meaning "she of the triple road," representing her dominance over the crossroads.

She also has many titles attributed to her.

- **Nyktypolos:** Meaning "she who wanders at night," associated with her role as the goddess of witchcraft and magic
- **Chthoniē:** Meaning "chthonic," which symbolizes her role as the goddess of the underworld
- **Skylakagetis:** Meaning "leader of the dogs," which is also associated with her role as the goddess of witchcraft
- **Trioditis:** Meaning "she of the triple road," representing her role as the goddess of the underworld

- **Sōteira:** Meaning "savior," showcasing how she helps needy people
- **Other titles that reflect her good nature are:** "Kourotrophos," which means "nurse of the young," and "atalos," which means tender

The Depiction of Hekate

In the very first depiction of Hekate, she was portrayed like any other goddess at the time, seated and wearing modest attire. Later, she was depicted in various sculptures as a female figure with three bodies and three heads to signify her role as the guardian of the crossroads, with each one of her sides guarding one of the roads.

Hekate's Family

Hekate is the daughter of Asteria, the Titan goddess of nighttime divinations and falling stars; Perses, the Titan god of destruction; the granddaughter of Coeus, the Titan of intelligence; and Phoebe, the Titan of bright intellect and the moon. However, the Greek author Euripides believed that her mother was Leto, the goddess of motherhood. In other legends, she is portrayed as the daughter of Zeus, the chief deity and god of the sky, Demeter, the goddess of the harvest, or Zeus and Nyx, the goddess of the night. Others considered Hera, the goddess of women, to be her mother. However, it is believed that Hesiod portrayed the most accurate version of her heritage in his poem describing Asteria and Perses as her parents.

Her strongest association is with Demeter, who some often liken to Hekate. This close connection results from the close relationships both goddesses developed when Hekate helped Demeter find her daughter.

Although she is often portrayed as a virgin like Artemis and Athena, some legends state that she is the mother of the witch Medea, the monster Scylla, and other mythical creatures.

Hekate throughout History

Anatolia (modern-day Turkey) was closely connected to Greece, and both countries experienced cultural exchange through migration, colonization, and trade. They also borrowed legends and deities from one another. It is believed that Hekate originated from Caria in Anatolia, and the ancient Greeks borrowed her and incorporated her into their pantheon of gods. Hekate had many followers in Caria, and she was the main deity in some towns.

The Greeks adopted Hekate into their mythology during the Archaic Period, where she underwent multiple transformations. Homer wasn't familiar with Hekate, so she didn't appear in Greek mythology until the Greek poet Hesiod first mentioned her in his poem Theogony. Hesiod didn't portray her as the goddess of the underworld or magic. However, he showed her as highly respected among the pantheon of the gods, with Zeus honoring and holding her in very high regard. In his poem, Hekate was the goddess of the sky, sea, and Earth, with no association with death or the underworld. She was a helpful goddess to the rich and poor, the weak and the strong.

In the fifth century, Hekate's portrayal was far from how Hesiod described her in early literature. She became known as a menacing and dark goddess. However, the Greek poet Pindar mentioned her soft side by describing her as "a friendly virgin." She was also accompanied by Erinyes or the Furies (deities of vengeance), who punished those who committed evil deeds. Her children, the Empusae (female demons), walked around seducing men.

Only in the fifth century did she begin having a more prominent role in Greek mythology. Before that, she played supporting roles in other goddesses' stories, like Artemis, the goddess of hunting and wild animals, Persephone, and Demeter.

To this day, she is still portrayed as the goddess of witchcraft and the underworld. However, no one knows why she has undergone this shift.

In the sixth century, Hekate was portrayed in a very different image. She was regarded as a cosmic soul or an entity that could be invoked by contemplating or practicing certain rituals.

No one knows when exactly people began to worship Hekate. Like many other Greek deities, she existed before written mythology. Ancient cultures passed down their stories orally from one generation to the next. Since there weren't source materials, these stories underwent many changes. People often added or omitted certain details until they differed from the original stories.

Although Hekate wasn't featured in Homer's epic poems, her daughter Circe did appear. In Odysseus, a sea witch called Circe plays a considerable role. Odysseus would seek her counsel so he and his men could safely cross the sea. She was described as an enchantress who could curse anyone who crossed her into beasts; she was also an expert in magic, just like her mother.

Hekate was featured in many works of literature as well. William Shakespeare mentioned her in association with strange rituals and dark magic.

The Goddess

In Greek mythology, Hekate is the goddess of doorways, crossroads, magic, witchcraft, the Moon, agriculture, marriage, childbirth, ghosts, hellhounds, and other creatures of the night. She played a role in everything that concerned mankind, whether in life or death. However, Hekate was considered mainly a witchcraft and magic goddess during the fifth century. She is also associated with necromancy and the occult.

She greatly influences both the world of the living and the dead. Her dominion over necromancy and ghosts result from her ability to move between the realms. She also chooses the souls who can travel to and from the underworld, giving her the power to raise the dead and call on spirits. Whenever she roams the Earth, she is often accompanied by the souls of childless and unmarried women. Moving between different worlds was a recurring theme in Hekate's life since she was born in the realm of Titans, yet she found her place in the Olympian pantheon among the Greek gods.

She is a very powerful and mysterious goddess. One can't classify her as a good or evil goddess since she is capable of both. Some can flinch at the mention of her name, while others find her a safe haven that provides justice and protection.

However, this doesn't mean that Hekate should be feared. Her association with magic and witchcraft gives her the reputation of a sinister and terrifying goddess. The Greek author Hesiod, one of the first people to mention her in classical literature, described her as a kindhearted goddess who always provides help to those who call on her.

Hekate is also the goddess of boundaries like borders, city walls, or doorways. The most significant boundary in Greek mythology is the one between life and death. The ancient Greeks believed that the spirits of the dead crossed over this boundary to reach the other world. Hekate can be described as a veil separating both worlds while she stands guard in the middle watching over the living and the dead.

Hekate and Witchcraft

The Romans and the Greeks worshiped Hekate as the goddess of witches. In the story of the Greek hero Jason and his heroic men, the Argonauts, who went on many adventures together, they sought the help of the witch Medea, one of Hekate's devotees and followers, to help them on their journey. The Hellenistic poet Theocritus also told the story of Simaetha, who invoked Hekate to bring back her lover Delphis.

Although Hekate is a protective deity and the goddess of boundaries, her most popular association is with magic. No one knows the origin of Hekate's transition to witchcraft, seeing as she first appeared as a kind goddess connected with light aspects. However, it is believed that she became associated with magic when her powers evolved, and she could grant favors to her followers. Being the goddess of all boundaries, including that between the supernatural and the natural, contributed to turning her into the goddess of witchcraft.

She became a dark witch due to her connection with the underworld. Since she could freely move between worlds, she could uncover secrets of the living and dead.

Hekate shared her knowledge of magic with her devoted followers like Medea.

The Protector

Hekate is a protective goddess because of her role as the guardian of doorways and borders. She watches over cities and homes to prevent evil from passing through. She was often referred to as Apotropaia, which meant "to turn away," which symbolizes her role in protecting places. There is even a type of magic called apotropaic, inspired by the goddess, protecting homes from harm and evil. Even her dogs play a protective role. They acted as watchdogs by barking to warn homeowners of intruders or danger.

She doesn't just keep evil out, but she also allows it to pass through and enter homes. If you anger or disrespect the goddess, she allows bad luck and evil into their homes. Hesiod mentioned in his poem that Hekate had the power to allow or deny misfortune.

Hekate Cults

The Greek geographer Pausanias stated that Hekate had many cults in her name on various Greek islands. For instance, a mysterious cult in Aegina worshiped the goddess and believed she could heal mental illness. In other islands like Miletos, Erythrai, Thessaly, Kos, and Samothrace, many cults were dedicated to Hekate, where her followers built altars and presented sacrifices in her honor. The goddess was also worshiped during the Roman and Hellenistic eras.

Hekate was worshiped in many other places worldwide, with various cults worshiping her privately or publicly.

Hekate in Other Cultures

Hekate wasn't only popular among the Greeks and Romans, but many other ancient cultures called on her when they needed help with witchcraft. In ancient Egypt, a magical papyrus containing various spells and magical texts associated with Hekate was discovered. However, she was referred to by other names like Selene, Persephone, Brimo, and Baubo.

Hekate in Greek Mythology

One can't truly know Hekate or her personality without learning about her roles in Greek myths.

The Abduction of Persephone

Hades was in love with his beautiful niece Persephone. He knew her mother, Demeter was protective of her and would never give her hand in marriage to anyone. So, one day, he decided to kidnap her. As Persephone walked around the field smelling flowers, Hades climbed up from the underworld in a chariot and abducted her. Persephone was terrified and screaming, and the only one who heard her cry for help was Hekate.

After losing her daughter, Demeter was devastated and looked for her everywhere on Earth. Hekate came to her and explained that she heard Persephone screaming, but she didn't know who had taken her. Hekate suggested that Demeter would go to Helios (the sun god) to seek his help as he could see everything that happened on Earth. Helios told Demeter that Hades was the one who abducted her daughter.

Demeter was depressed and ignored her duties. As the goddess of agriculture, she abandoned the lands and crops, leaving mankind to starve. However, Hekate didn't leave her side and was her loyal companion until her daughter returned.

Zeus, Demeter's husband and Persephone's father, interfered and returned his daughter. Hekate was very happy to have Persephone back and to see her reunited with her mother. She became Persephone's attendant and accompanied her to the underworld. If it weren't for Hekate, Demeter would have never been able to find her daughter. She was also honored and highly respected in the cults of Persephone and Demeter for reuniting the mother and daughter. This incident also earned Hekate the epithet "sōteira."

Zeus's Birth

Various myths tell the story of the birth of Zeus. In one version, Cronus (the god of time, king of the Titans, and Zeus's father) feared that his children would one day grow up and overthrow him. So, to protect himself, he swallowed them all after they were born. When his wife Rhea, the mother goddess, gave birth to their youngest, Zeus, she didn't want him to meet the same fate as her other children. She put a stone in clothes to resemble her newborn son and gave it to Hekate to bring to Cronus, who would swallow it instead of Zeus, who Rhea kept safe.

Zeus
https://pixabay.com/es/illustrations/zeus-mitolog%c3%ada-dios-griego-zeus-7683518/

This story shows Hekate as courageous, for who would dare to play a ruse on the king of Titans unless they were bold and fearless?

The Attack on the Olympians

One day, the Giants attacked the Olympians (the main deities of the Greek pantheon). Hekate fought with the Olympians, and she managed to kill Clytius, one of the giants and the son of the Earth goddess Gaia. After helping the gods win the war, Hekate was highly revered by Zeus and all the other deities. Everyone saw her as a powerful goddess who they should never underestimate.

This shows Hekate as a brave and powerful warrior who would never shy away from a battle.

Hekate in Modern Times

Nowadays, Hekate is mainly known as the dark goddess of witchcraft associated with ghosts. Although she doesn't make many appearances in modern Greek mythology, she plays a big role in Wicca, neopaganism, and modern witchcraft. The Triple Goddess, worshiped by many neopagans, is believed to be Hekate, who also has a triple form.

The Contradictions and Mysteries of Hekate

It is believed that Hekate is the most misunderstood deity in Greek mythology – and this makes sense since she is the subject of many contradictions throughout history. She is portrayed as a guardian, protector of homes, and the goddess of witchcraft and the underworld. She can offer protection from harm yet allow evil and misfortune into people's lives. She is both a foreign and a Greek deity.

No one can understand the powers or origins of Hekate, especially since they underwent many changes in Greek mythology. Some scholars argue that Hekate is a different goddess than the one people are familiar with now. Since her name is derived from Apollo's other name, Hecatos, Hekate is believed to be another name for Artemis, Apollo's twin sister. As more and more people started to worship Artemis in ancient Greece, her followers noticed her many positive attributes. However, like any other deity, she has negative qualities as well. Her devotees separated the dark side of her personality to create a different goddess and gave her the name Hekate.

Although Hekate is known for being a witch associated with darkness and magic, many of her legends portray her positively, whether it was helping Demeter find Persephone or fighting alongside the Greek gods. On the other hand, some stories showed the goddess's dark side. In one story, there was a witch called Gale, who Hekate cursed and turned into a polecat because she found her behavior and desires unnatural.

Some scholars believe that Hekate is associated with the ancient Egyptian goddess of fertility Heqet who was linked to magic, which they called *heqa*.

Although various myths state that Hekate was the daughter of either gods or giants, some legends portray her as a mortal. According to some works of literature, she was a princess called Iphigenia who was about to die when Artemis saved her and transformed her into a goddess.

One can struggle to fully understand or define Hekate. She is one of few Greek deities who weren't featured in Homer's "The Iliad" or "The Odyssey," which is why little is known about her. However, she has appeared in various myths as the goddess of households, agriculture, witches, travel crossroads, and many others.

Hekate has always been surrounded by mystery, whether it's her origin or powers. She first appeared as the goddess of the sky with no association with witchcraft and – out of nowhere – her image changed as if she had become a different goddess.

Once again, we ask: who is Hekate, honestly? Is she a good or evil goddess? Answering this question isn't so simple. Every person has a definition of good and evil. Some would consider an action evil, while others may justify it. Hekate is just like human beings. She has positive and negative traits and is capable of wrongdoing. One can describe her as neutral. As the goddess of crossroads and boundaries, she stands between the living and the dead, and the natural and supernatural, so she is capable of good and evil.

In other words, she stands in a middle ground between two extremes, refusing to choose a side. You can choose how you want to view Hekate. However, one can argue that she is a feminist icon. She is portrayed in many of her legends as a strong, brave goddess who protects those who need her. Yet, she can't tolerate injustice or disrespect. She is an intriguing figure that you can't help but look up to and admire. Her kindness and darkness make her a goddess with human qualities that anyone can relate to her. The mystery and contradictions around Hekate are part of her appeal. She can pose more questions than answers, but her personality has two aspects, lightness and darkness, good and evil.

Who Hekate really is can be open to many interpretations, with your personal view impacting how you see her.

Chapter 2: The Hekatean Witch

Now that you've learned who Hekate is, you can delve into what a Hekatean witch is. This chapter provides recommendations on how to know you're drawn to Hekate and to what degree. You'll receive guidance on the broad range of ways the Hekatean witch works with the goddess, including the practice of finding one's own truth and receiving clarity when you're at a crossroads.

Being a Hekatean witch means following the path of the goddess.
https://unsplash.com/photos/43NPCi0NJlY

Hallmarks of a Hekatean Witch

Being a Hekatean witch means claiming the path of following the goddess - on whatever journey she takes you on. Honoring her requires much work, as she is considered the Queen of witches. It includes venerating her regularly, invoking her for spiritual healing and assistance for growth, and building a connection with her. The Hekatean witch also honors all her fellow Hekate devotees - living or dead. In modern times, there is plenty of information available on the goddess. Unfortunately, some of it is rooted in misconceptions, which makes many curious spiritual and magical seekers hesitant to work with Hekate. A true devotee takes the time to delve into the ancient Greek lore of the goddess and the famous witches who venerated her. Through this pursuit, they understand how to reach out to the goddess and how she can help them.

As a Hekatean witch, you might also enjoy practicing her craft by reviving ancient Greek magic and incorporating it into your modern practices. A witch can choose many ways to venerate the goddess, including meditation, candle rituals, and herbalism. Many Hekatean witches are drawn to a natural lifestyle, preferring to use plants as natural remedies than treating conditions with modern medicine. They use various types and parts of herbs and ask Hekate for help when preparing them for treatments. Another characteristic of Hekatean devotees is a deep reverence for the balance of life and death. Instead of viewing death as the end of life, the devotees acknowledge death as a transitional period. Those crossing the liminal space must be honored through rituals and ceremonies. Dead ancestors gathered wisdom and passed it down to the new generations, for which they earned Hekate's respect. She helped them through their transitional periods, in life and in death. By celebrating the dead, you're honoring Hekate too. If you feel the need to honor your ancestors during transitional periods, it can be a great sign that you're ready to become a Hekatean witch. Liminal periods and spaces represent an in-between. For example, dusk is a liminal period between day and night. Samhain is a period dividing summer and winter. During these times, the divide between the world of the living and the spiritual realm is weaker, so it is natural to feel the pull towards the goddess and the dead souls she represents. You can feel drawn to family members, friends who've passed, or long-dead ancestors whose wisdom you can tap into during magical and spiritual practices. A witch will venerate all dead, make offerings, and ask for their blessing for magical work.

Hekate is known for her warm and kind nature - but she carries dark wisdom. True devotees understand that she has the power to cause harm. As long as you seek her out with the right intentions in mind, she will do you no harm. However, if your purpose is not pure, nothing good will come of working with her. For a Hekatean witch, the goddess represents the ultimate balance. They strive to obtain this balance by honoring the goddess through learning different practices.

The Hekatean witch knows that the goddess can only help those who wish to live a good life. Living one's life well means being aware of one's desires, strengths, and weaknesses. She can only help those who are helping themselves. She is there for those seeking their truth and wanting to find their authentic voices. True devotees will always make sure that their intentions are clear when calling on Hekate and take their time preparing for their magical or spiritual work. They know how crucial it is to be in a proper head space.

For a Hekatean witch, working with the goddess means seeking personal power. They know that the goddess won't do anything for them; they have to find their own power to overcome the challenges they face. At the same time, they never fail to show her humility. Hekate calls on her devotees to recognize the part of her that resides in all beings. She wants you to acknowledge that your soul comes from her essence. However, she also prompts you to find your own truths - your own spiritual path. As the goddess of balance, Hekate teaches you that there are times you need to be confident and stand up for yourself, establishing boundaries and stopping anyone who wishes to harm you. At other times, she will warn you to remain humble and look at challenges as opportunities for spiritual growth instead of insurmountable obstacles. If you feel that you should strive to be balanced like Hekate is, you're on the right path to becoming a true devotee.

A Hekatean witch seeks to celebrate and worship Hekate by being willing to put aside any prejudice, become her student, and accept her guidance. Many of her devotees express themselves through art and other creative endeavors. This allows them to connect with the goddess and draw on her powers to empower their practices. It allows them to obtain balance and resilience at the same time.

Devotees of Hekate are creative because her power guides them. They know how to express themselves through her symbols and many other spiritual and magical tools. They can find these everywhere. Staying true to one of Hekate's fundamental teachings, if you help yourself, she will be able to help you. For example, instead of using actual crossroads and liminal spaces, a Hekatean witch will create symbols of these from everyday items and situations.

Remember that all the above practices, beliefs, and pursuits are generalized descriptions of approaches used by Hekate devotees and priestesses. However, like any Hekate witch will tell you, working with the goddess is a highly personal process. Feel free to take inspiration from these practices and beliefs, but only embark on those that feel right for you. For your connection with the goddess to grow truly powerful, you must find your unique way of bonding with her and expressing your intentions and gratitude.

Signs That Hekate Is Calling on You

The goddess is known for letting her presence known but is very careful about timing. A Hekatean witch knows that the goddess will only call on you when you need her and are ready for her help. You won't have to seek her out, nor does it do you any good to do so. As an ancient soul connected to all beings in the universe, she senses when she is needed. She knows when your life is thrown out of balance or when you're at a crossroads in life. If you are, she will come. If not, she won't help you. When she arrives, she will announce her presence with bold signs. She is an active deity - which is one of the main reasons she remains in the lives of her followers and is revered by many. Once you've established a connection with her and have begun nurturing your bond, she will keep reaching out to you. She will continue to guide you on your transitional journey as long as you need her.

According to certain beliefs, for Hekate to reach out to you, you must first ask for a sign from her. However, this isn't always the case. If you've never worked with her before, you can't ask for signs of her presence. However, she can present herself in symbolic messages. This is because, while you might remember asking her for help consciously, you might have actually done it intuitively. Intuition is a force with the power to make spiritual connections you aren't even aware of. To make sure that their goddess is contacting them, Hekatean witches often made offerings to ask if she was sending messages. They consider any signs they receive after completing the offering a confirmation.

The most common signs of Hekate reaching out to a witch or practitioner is seeing black or wild dogs. This might be a vision of a wild animal, like a coyote, feral dog, wolf, and fox. A black dog might even run up to you and try to make contact with you. If the dog's owner says that the animal rarely lets anyone pet them or go near them, this is a sure sign of Hekate inviting a witch on a journey. Hekatean witches also believe that hearing dogs barking (especially if the source is unknown) is also a sign of reaching out to them. It is believed that these are the sounds of deceased animals she used to communicate with her followers.

Seeing snakes is also a veritable sign of Hekate communicating with a devotee. These creatures are associated with magic, so if you have visions of them during your magical work, these might be messages from the goddess. Hekatean witches know that just as the goddess lives near the surface of the spiritual world, the snakes live near the surface of the ground. However, these animals tend to stay away from people, so there is typically a good reason for seeing them.

If you see keys, thresholds, doorways, torches, or lights, you're likely a Hekatean witch ready to embark on a long journey with the goddess. Finding old keys signals that you are about to cross a threshold that'll bring great changes into your life. Seeing how she is known as the light bearer, Hekate often communicates through light. In modern times, this will be through flickering streetlights and not torches. Still, if you see one flickering in multiples of three, you're about to receive a powerful message from Hekate.

Changes in temperature around you can also indicate that the goddess is near. Her world is a dark and cold place. You can feel when she reaches out to you from a liminal space by sensing a chill. You can also have a vision or dream in which the world around you becomes darker (even in the daytime) as if the sun has never fully risen.

Be Careful When Working with Hekate

Hekatean witches believe their mistress isn't a deity to be taken lightly. She might not be the scary creature bringing death like some modern interpretations want to portray her, but this doesn't mean you can ask her for frivolous requests. She can help you transform your life - but only if you're truly ready to make meaningful changes. For instance, if your idea of transformation is landing a high-paying job, winning the lottery, or getting back with your ex, Hekate isn't the deity that can help you. While she won't retaliate for being asked these requests, you'll waste your time and resources because your work with her will be fruitless. On the other hand, if you wish to transform your life because you feel stuck or lost in a dark space, she might be able to guide you. It's all about wanting to find your own truth - and never about making or expecting miracles.

At this point, you might wonder how you'll know if you're ready for Hekate's help and how to ask her to find your truths. The first sign is your willingness to reach out and ask questions. It means you're aware that you're at a crossroads or in any other situation from which empowerment through Hekate can help you move forward. Next, you must accept that she is the goddess of change - not some dark witch who can retaliate if you don't act in a certain way. True spiritual conversions are rarely smooth. They're usually messy and painful. They require people to give up something, to leave comforting habits behind - and a true Hekaten witch knows and embraces this knowledge. If you reach out and your transformation begins, you must accept the pain that comes with it with humility. The witch never blames her mistress for the pain because she knows happiness can't be reached without it.

The next sign that you're ready for Hekate's help is that you're willing to open your mind to the messages you'll receive from her. Before you reach out, do a little introspection to see if you're ready for what it takes. Don't waste your time inviting Hekate into your space if you aren't. However, if you can adopt a mindset that welcomes transformation, you'll be good to go. This involves expressing gratitude for the blessing and lessons you've received so far, no matter how challenging the latter ones were. You can only move onto the next stage of life well lived if you already feel you've begun it. Affirmations about positive experiences and achievements often reassure you that you're doing good. The goddess is waiting for you to acknowledge that you're deserving. Once you do, she will send more signs and advice your way.

If you are ready to accept that Hekate will only be your guide while you do the hard work, you'll be even more empowered. Her power might be in you, but you control it, just as you control your emotions, thoughts, and actions. It's you who will be transforming your own life. The goddess will only assist you on your journey, occasionally steering you in the right direction if needed. You must accept responsibility and accountability for your actions and life. Your spiritual transformation will be your journey; you must gain self-awareness before it begins. You can't expect it to be easy, but you can help yourself by accepting it as a truth. With this approach, you'll be able to embrace the change, even if it comes in a way you've never expected it to arrive. This is what it means to speak your authentic voice. It's having faith in your power and not expecting someone else to do the work for you. Remember, she is all about telling as it is. She won't have anyone tell her she can't do something, nor should you.

Despite the painful changes that come with it, transformation can be beautiful. You'll know you're ready when you begin to act consciously. Instead of talking or daydreaming about changing your life, you're actually doing something that will start this process. This is when Hekate will step in. Because she won't help those who remain inactive, fearful of taking the first step, she will only guide those ready to move forward with their lives. She knows it's hard to leave the comfort and the known variables of your life behind - but she also knows it's necessary.

Some novices wonder whether Hekate will like them, often fearing that she will refuse their requests for assistance. When in fact, Hekate wants you to like yourself. She wants you to feel worthy of the positive transformation. You'll have no trouble communicating and bonding with her if you speak your mind and express your true desires. Hekate won't expect you to be perfect and not make any mistakes along your journey. After all, that's why she comes to your aid, to whisper her guidance as you work yourself through the messy and mistake-ridden transformation process. Hekate's authentic path is imperfect, *and this is what she is asking you to embrace.*

By embarking on her path, you've acknowledged that you'll accept any changes she brings. These will come in the form of spiritual messages, allowing you to know yourself better. You'll learn to identify your personal boundaries, a truly empowering effect of becoming a Hekatean devotee. You'll be able to say no when necessary – without justifying your words and actions. Hekate won't be responsible for this - you will. She will only push you to find your inner voice and the trigger you need to release it. Gaining self-awareness, self-confidence, and the ability to get in touch with your intuition even before you delve into in-depth work with the goddess are crucial achievements. They all signal you're ready to begin your journey as a Hekatean witch.

The last sign that you're ready to reach out to Hekate is that you accept that the goddess knows you better than you know yourself. You might be able to lie to yourself about wanting your life to go in a specific direction, but you won't be able to fool her. In these modern times, societal norms and financial obligations often create misleading desires. They can make you believe you can transform your life by having more money or becoming famous for the wrong reasons. However, the goddess knows that none of this is true, and you'll have to learn to listen to her.

If - after reading through all these signs - you still don't feel ready to start working with Hekate, don't worry. Take the time to learn what you truly want to do, and reach out to her when ready. She has been around for a long time and will continue to do so. She will wait for you until you're prepared to work with her. When *you do* start working with her, don't feel rushed to find your own truth. It's a long process that takes a lot of practice and intuitive work.

How Strong Is Your Connection to Hekate?

Now that you know how the Hekatean witch follows her patroness and how to tell if the goddess is calling on you, you can learn more about how drawn you are to Hekate. The following quiz will help you glimpse at the level of your devotion and provide some pointers on how to go about your practice:

1. I feel drawn to Hekate during liminal periods, like when the day turns into the night at dusk or the summer transitions into winter during the fall.
2. I feel a deep desire to celebrate death as a transitional period knowing that life goes on beyond it.
3. I want to learn more about honoring Hekate and connecting with her.
4. I see signs of the goddess calling on me, sending me images of keys, black dogs, snakes, and death symbols.
5. I want to explore how to venerate Hekate through daily rituals.
6. I want to celebrate Hekate by visiting her temples and participating in rituals with other devotees.
7. I feel I am about to arrive at a crossroads, and Hekate can guide me through this transitional period.

8. I am ready to make changes in my life, accepting that if I ask Hekate for help, the changes will be powerful and perhaps painful.
9. Despite her might, I don't fear Hekate but revere her beauty and power, allowing her to guide me toward a better life.

The Results

- You are simply curious if you've identified with only 1-3 of 9 statements. You've heard about Hekate and wish to explore more but aren't sure if following her is the right path for you. Continue your research to see if you can get inspired to forge your unique bond with the goddess and use her aid to transform your life.
- You are considered a true devotee if you've identified yourself with 4-6 out of 9 statements. You wish to honor Hekate and what she represents through regular practices. You're sure that she is the one who can help you live a better life, and you're ready to take on the challenges she brings forth to facilitate your transformation. Continue celebrating at her altar through small rituals fortifying your connection to her.
- If you've identified yourself with 7-9 of 9 statements - you are as devoted to Hekate as a priestess. You are ready to embrace the goddess in her every form and trust her implicitly. You accept that Hekate is everywhere and will know how to help when you need her assistance. You're inspired to devote a significant part of your life to Hekate and give into her transformative powers.

Chapter 3: Hekate's Signs and Symbols

All gods and goddesses have signs and symbols associated with them. Often, these symbols are shown in illustrations or sculptures like the keys, dogs, and torches, usually depicted with Hekate. Since the goddess is associated with the night, many of her symbols are related to dark elements like the underworld and death. However, Hekate is also a mysterious goddess with many contradictions, so you will also find some symbols associated with light.

This chapter will cover all the different symbols of Hekate and their meanings.

Hekate's Wheel

Hekate's wheel is also called the Strophalos of Hekate. It is a Wiccan symbol that belongs to the Dianic Traditions and Hellenic Recon. The wheel is a visual representation of Hekate. It consists of a six-sided star inside a circle surrounded by a labyrinth with three sides and another circle. The symbol first emerged in the first century when it was depicted with Hekate.

Hekate's Wheel.

However, some scholars believe these first images of the wheel were with Aphrodite, the goddess of love. Still, both images of the goddesses ended up overlapping.

Hekate is associated with the concept of the Trinity. She was first the goddess of the sea, sky, and earth. After she became associated with magic, she was depicted as a triple goddess with either three heads and one body, three bodies and one head, or three heads and three bodies. She is also associated with the three aspects of women's lives the maiden, mother, and crone. Hekate is usually referred to as the "Triple Moon Goddess" because she also represents the three different phases of the moon. The aspect of the trinity is a part of Hekate's identity, and it is apparent in the three sides of the labyrinth.

Although each part of the wheel has its own meaning, the symbol itself represents the transfer of energy and knowledge through divine forces. The Strophalos of Hekate are connected to the Chaldean Oracles, associated with the Neoplatonic metaphysical belief. This belief states that an all-knowing and all-powerful Father with unlimited divine powers and intellect created the universe. He is the main source of all wisdom in the cosmos.

This Father has his own ambassadors who are responsible for transmitting wisdom and knowledge to mankind. Hekate is one of his emissaries who delivers this information to Earth so everyone can benefit from it. Each part of the symbol has a different meaning related to this transmission of knowledge.

The Labyrinth

The labyrinth symbolizes the different stages of human life that every person must go through. During this journey, one should absorb the knowledge of the universe before their life ends and their spirit returns to its Maker. The labyrinth also represents the self-discovery that one undergoes in life. It can also be described as a loop that signifies the circle of life and its three stages.p

Life

The first cycle is life, and it represents birth. The spirit spends this stage bound to the physical body.

Death

The second cycle is death. It happens after the physical body withers and is separated from the spirit. The spirit then ascends to a different plane of existence, the realm of the dead, where it spends the rest of eternity.

Rebirth

The last stage is rebirth. After the spirit ascends, it can reach a higher state of being and experience enlightenment. The spirit should then go through a rebirth where it either reincarnates and lives again in the physical form or returns to its Divine Father.

The Star

The star is another part of the Hekate. It is placed in the center and represents the Divine Father, who is omniscient and the source of all knowledge. The six sides of the star symbolize the spark that ignites in one's soul and connects you to the world around you and the Divine Father.

There are other forms of the wheel with the letters X or Y at its center instead of the star. The letter Y represents the intersection of the three crossroads where Hekate stands guard in her Triple Goddess form.

The Inner Circle

The inner circle is the first circle in the Hekate wheel. It symbolizes the goddess herself, who is the guardian and protector of divine knowledge and the one who distributes it among mankind by being a reflection of the divinity of the Creator.

The Outer Circle

The second circle and the last part of the wheel form the outer circle, symbolizing the limitations of the energy Hekate uses when transferring Divine knowledge to humans. An enclosed area between the two circles represents the space between the intellectual and physical worlds. Hekate uses this space to spread the Divine information.

The wheel also symbolizes the concepts of renewal and rebirth since it is related to the shape of the labyrinthine serpent, which rotates in a spiral form. In Greek mythology, the serpent has different meanings and is often depicted with other deities. For instance, snakes are engraved on the staves of Asclepius, the god of medicine, and Hermes, the god of fertility and language, representing medicine and healing.

Hekate is also often depicted with snakes which symbolize fertility and rebirth. In one of the ancient Greek creation myths, the world was created by a giant snake that incubated an egg. Snakes shed their skin every few years and come out with new and rejuvenated bodies. For this reason, serpents represent rebirth and the idea that every creature can be reborn differently.

The spiral part of the symbol is responsible for transmitting Divine knowledge to mankind through rituals like turning the wheels of the Strophalos to release a sound. If one performs this ritual after the death of someone, Hekate will respond to this sound and come down to help the spirit of the deceased ascend to the Divine Father.

The spiral and other parts of the Strophalos are associated with rituals related to the Divine. They usually attract the Divine Father and Hekate and can also be used to perform various spells. The sound it releases resembles the movements and sounds of the iynges, enchanting mediums and tools connected with the Divine intellect.

Using the Hekate Wheel

The Hekate wheel is one of the major symbols of the goddess since it is used to call on her and invoke her powers. It is a very popular symbol among Wiccans and Neopagans. Hekate represents feminine energy because of its association with the three stages of womanhood and the moon's energy. For this reason, women can invoke the goddess during any stage of their lives.

Besides being a symbol of divine knowledge, the wheel also represents the journey of the human spirit. Each person must go through each part of the symbol by experiencing the ups, downs, and complexities of life under the guidance and protection of Hekate until one reaches the final stage, which is the center of the wheel, and finally achieve enlightenment.

Nowadays, people use the Hekate wheel for religious purposes. Practitioners of various religions, like Hellenic Reconstructionism, a Neopagan tradition inspired by ancient Greek beliefs, also incorporate the wheel into their practices. Many women also wear the wheel as jewelry, like necklaces or bracelets, or even have them tattooed on their bodies because they believe it can bring wealth, success, and good luck into their lives by creating a connection between them and Hekate.

Facts about the Hekate Wheel

- If you see someone wearing the wheel, they are probably practitioners of the Dianic Traditions of Wicca.
- Many feminists also wear or use the wheel because it is associated with the Triple Goddess and the three stages of femininity.
- The three parts in the labyrinth always look as if they are rotating. This represents drawing forward one's psyche to connect with Divine wisdom.
- The wheel is sometimes called "*iynx*," and one can use it as a divinatory tool, a devotional wheel, or to bring love into their life.
- Sometimes, devotees place the wheel over their heads and let it whirl to create a sound that drives predators away and increases their awareness.
- Essentially, the wheel serves as a reminder that Hekate is by your side, guiding you through your journey in the physical world.

The Hekate Wheel and the Iynx

Although iynx is another name for the Hekate wheel, some argue that the two are different symbols associated with the goddess. "Iynx" is derived from "*iunx,*" Greek for the *wryneck bird,* a type of woodpecker bird that feeds on ants. Originally, people used the iynx wheel to perform spells. The wheel's rotation makes a sound similar to an iunx's call.

The iynx wheel is associated with Aphrodite and her son Eros, more commonly known as Cupid and the god of physical desire and passion. Both used the wheel to attract lovers and bring them together. The iynx is also associated with Hekate, as is clear in one of the poems by the Greek poet Theocritus. He told the story of a woman who went to a sorcerer and asked him to return her unfaithful lover. The practitioner used the iynx wheel to cast the spell and invoked Hekate.

Understandably, you can be confused when Hekate is called on in love spells since she has dominion over aspects unrelated to romance. However, many stories in Greek mythology and literature talk about how the goddess was called on to assist with matters of the heart.

The iynx wheel is also associated with funerals and death, another reason it's considered a symbol for Hekate.

Dogs

Hekate is often portrayed with dogs. In Greek mythology, dogs would bark at night to announce the goddess's arrival on Earth. They also howl when she or any of her followers use magic. She can even take the form of a dog.

Hekate's dogs were first depicted as quiet and friendly creatures. However, just like the goddess underwent some changes through the years, so did her pets. They came to represent angry spirits or demons. Similar to the mysterious shift in Hekate, no one knows exactly why the depictions of her dogs also changed.

One can say that the dogs resemble Hekate as they also have dark and light sides. They can be dangerous and scary creatures or provide assistance and protection.

One of her dogs was originally the Trojan queen Hecuba. After Troy fell, Hecuba was captured, thrown off a cliff, and died instantly. Hekate felt sorry for the dead queen and brought her back to life as a dog who became a loyal companion to the goddess for eternity.

Hekate is also associated with other animals like:
- Boars
- Snakes
- Bats
- Lambs
- Sheep
- Horses

Polecat

Hekate is associated with polecats, and she is usually depicted with them. The reason behind this association goes back to an old legend that tells the story of Heracles' (the divine hero) birth.

One of Zeus's mortal lovers, Alcmene, was pregnant with his son Heracles. When his wife Hera found out, she was very jealous and wanted to get rid of the child before he was born. She sent the Moirae Sisters (the Fates) and Eileithyia, the goddess of childbirth, to close off Alcmene's womb. When her handmaid, Galinthias, discovered what the goddesses did, she lied to them by saying that Alcmene had already given birth. Moirae and Eileithyia fell for the trick and let go of their hold on Alcmene's womb, and she gave birth. They punished her by turning her into a polecat when they found out that Galinthias lied to them.

Galinthias led a terrible life as a polecat. She had to hide in dirty holes and struggled to survive. When Hekate learned about the poor maid's fate, she sympathized with her. She tried to reverse the curse but failed, making the polecat one of her sacred attendants.

Keys

Hekate is often depicted holding keys, and because of that, she is described as the keeper of keys. These are believed to be the keys to the universe that can unlock its mysteries, magic, and healing powers. Other scholars argue that these are the keys to the crossroads. Since she is the goddess of the crossroads and stands guard over them, she holds these keys to provide protection and prevent danger from entering. They are also believed to be the keys to the underworld, where she has dominion. Hekate uses this key to unlock the mysteries of the afterlife and the secrets of the occult.

During certain rituals, Hekate priestesses often carry keys to represent the goddess's role as the keeper of keys.

Everyone uses keys to unlock their car, home, office, etc., and some even use keys in their decor or wear them as jewelry. If you consider these keys to be symbols of Hekate, you can constantly feel that she is with you and providing protection through one of her symbols.

Crossroads

Hekate is the goddess of the crossroads, so naturally, they are one of her symbols. Boundaries can cause limitations in your daily life and set obstacles you must overcome to grow. Hekate's role as the goddess of the crossroads is to mediate these boundaries.

Crossroads can also represent the many daily choices, like which road to take, which job to apply to, or which decisions to make. Crossroads are also associated with the future, present, and past. In her triple form, Hekate can see each of the three crossroads, representing the past, present, and future. Therefore, she is in a perfect position to provide guidance and help one make better choices.

Triple Form

Hekate is a Triple goddess. Many of her statues and illustrations show her in her triple form. Like Hermes, the messenger of the gods, people placed her statues near borders and crossroads in ancient Greece to ward off misfortune, harm, and evil.

Daggers

In modern times and among Neo-pagans, Hekate is depicted with three torches, six arms, and sacred symbols: a dagger, rope, and a key. The dagger symbolizes the goddess's dominion over magic and witchcraft. It is also used to ward off evil spirits and perform ritualistic spells. For the followers of Hekate, the dagger can bring you to trust your inner voice and judgment, provide empowerment, and protect you from illusions.

Ropes

Hekate usually carries a rope, representing the umbilical cord, a symbol of renewal and rebirth. The rope is also called a scourge or a cord.

Triple Moon

As the triple moon goddess, Hekate is associated with the moon's dark side. If you remember from science class, the moon is a dark body, and its light reflects the sunlight. Hekate represents the moon's darkness in its true form, especially during the new moon phase.

Torches

Hekate is usually depicted holding two torches, one in each hand, to represent her role as a protector and provide guidance. She would light up the way for those struggling with obstacles and difficulties on their daily journey so they could see clearly and reach their destination.

Her torches were featured in a few legends. For instance, during the war between the Giants and the Olympian gods, she used her torch to kill the giant Clytius and help the gods win the war.

The torches are some of Hekate's most significant symbols, making her powerful and adding to her mysteries and contradictions. For a goddess associated with the dark aspects of life, like the underworld and the dark side of the moon, she is also a force of light.

One can always call on Hekate to light the darkness inside them or when they are facing obstacles and looking for someone to show them the way and illuminate their dark roads.

Serpents

In various illustrations, Hekate is depicted with a serpent in her hand. In ancient Greece, serpents were associated with necromancy and magic. People used them in spells to detect the presence of a spirit.

Crescent

The crescent has been a symbol of Hekate ever since Roman times. Back then, people saw her as mainly a moon goddess, so the crescent became her symbol to signify her connection with the moon.

Owls

In some illustrations, Hekate is depicted surrounded by owls which symbolize wisdom. Although she isn't the goddess of wisdom, she is still associated with it. For starters, as the goddess of the crossroads, she can see into the past, present, and future, possessing knowledge of each stage of one's life. She also has access to the Divine wisdom she spread among the people, so having owls as her symbol represents these different aspects of the goddess.

Willows

There are many symbols associated with willow trees. They signify survival, adaptability, hope, growth, change, and new beginnings. Since Hekate is the goddess of the crossroads, she represents new beginnings and change, which makes the willow tree her ideal symbol.

The goddess is associated with other plants as well.
- Pumpkins
- Currants
- Raisins
- Saffron
- Blackthorn
- Dark yew
- Groves of trees

Scents

Since Hekate is the goddess of the moon and is associated with night, she is often called the "Queen of the night." This makes the queen of the night flower an appropriate symbol of the goddess. The flowers are just as mysterious as Hekate because they bloom simultaneously, making them quite intriguing. In some cultures, if you pray to a deity or make a wish while the queen of the night is blooming, your wish or prayer will come true.

Other scents that are associated with Hekate:
- Lemon verbena
- Lime
- Honey
- Mugwort
- Myrrh
- Cinnamon

Colors

Hekate is associated with the color black. This makes sense for a goddess who represents the night, darkness, the underworld, and death. Black is also a mysterious color, so it perfectly fits the intriguing goddess.

Hekate is also associated with red-orange, yellow-orange, and orange.

Metals and Gems

Luminous and dark stones symbolize Hekate as they represent the dark aspects of the goddess's personality.

The gems and metals Hekate is associated with include:
- Smoky quartz
- Hematite

- Black onyx
- Black Tourmaline
- Moonstone
- Gold
- Silver
- Sapphire

Practical Exercise

Now that you have become familiar with Hekate's symbols, *try drawing your own*. You can draw the wheel in any of its forms or create something from your imagination using any of her symbols. Don't use Google to find ideas; let your intuition guide you instead and draw what feels right. Sit in a quiet room without distractions, get a blank piece of paper, hold a pen or pencil, and start drawing.

The symbols of Hekate reflect the many contradictions and mysteries around the goddess. She is associated with dark colors and metals and the dark side of the moon, yet she is depicted with a torch in her hand to provide light and guidance. Her symbols also showcase her significant role in one's life. She isn't only the goddess of witchcraft and the underworld. Still, she has the power to transfer Divine knowledge among mankind and can see into the future.

There are many sides to Hekate's personality and different aspects to worshiping her. One can use her symbols to cast spells, seek guidance, ask for protection, pray for wisdom, and various other things. Hecake is more than just a dark goddess associated with witchcraft; she can also be a force of light, helping you overcome obstacles and illuminating the darkest roads.

Chapter 4: Connecting with Hekate

You've now learned about Hekate and her associations; you're probably eager to make contact with her. This chapter will help you explore different methods of connecting – from journeying to her and meeting her at the crossroads to meditating with her and expressing your gratitude for her presence to mindfulness techniques that will bring the two of you together. You'll explore all the meaningful ways to bond with Hekate, preparing you for other practical techniques for working with the goddess (to be described in the subsequent chapters).

Important Disclaimers

Before you delve into the practical side of working with Hekate, you must consider a few things. The first one is your **mental health**. Witchcraft and rituals require intense focus and mental strength. Not only that, but working with Hekate also means that you'll experience changes in your life, which can make you vulnerable to negative influences. Remember, she is an incredibly powerful goddess and a witch who can land you plenty of spiritual and magical power - but you must be ready to accept it. You must be able to ward off the negative energies to overcome your difficulties.

All this is only possible if you have sound mental health. If you're already having issues with your mental health, you likely won't be able to focus on your intentions. In the best-case scenario, you won't be able to connect with Hekate. You'll only waste your mental energy when you could've used it for mental and spiritual healing. In the worst-case scenario, you'll have a bad experience (like disturbing visions and dreams), which will further contribute to the decline of your mental health.

So, if you've experienced mental health issues in the past, focus on healing before attempting to make contact with Hekate. Symptoms to watch out for include lack of sleep and other sleep disturbances, problems with memory, fatigue, depression, and anxiety. Furthermore, if you notice any of these symptoms after you've begun to work with Hekate, stop, and seek help from a medical professional to treat your symptoms. Don't continue until you've improved your mental well-being.

The next factor to consider is **fire safety.** Working with Hekacte often requires using candles, small torches, or other sources of fire. Never leave the flames unattended. If you're finished with them for a while and plan to leave the space, extinguish the fire. You can relight it when you return and dedicate time to supervise it again. Another reason you should leave flames burning for long periods is that the rituals you need them for require focus. You can focus on an intention for only so long - once your concentration declines, your work becomes ineffective. Relighting the flames is more effective when you return with a fresh mind and are ready to focus on your intention again. Avoid using open sources of fire near small children, pets, or in unventilated spaces. The focus the magical work requires can divert your attention from supervising the pets or children. This can prevent you from being able to stop them if they get too close to the flames. Working with flames in a ventilated space forms a better connection with Hekate. Not to mention it's much safer for you, your home, and those around you. Fire uses oxygen, which you'll also need. Working in a ventilated space will provide you with plenty of oxygen, and with all that oxygen cursing through your body and mind, you'll be able to focus better.

Lastly, you should keep in mind that working with Hekate requires **the use of herbs.** While the herbs the goddess uses have health benefits, they can also have adverse effects. Always consult a medical health professional before ingesting any herbs or using them topically. The same applies to essential oils, too - these contain herbal compounds in a concentrated form, so they can have an even greater impact on your health. When talking to your doctor, pharmacist, or an experienced herbalist about herbs or herbal blends you plan to use, mention if you have any pre-existing conditions. Some illnesses represent a contraindication for herbs used when working with Hekate. If you experience any side effects - such as skin irritations, nausea, or changes in breathing, blood pressure, or heart arrhythmia - after ingesting or topically applying the herbs, seek immediate medical attention. Stop using the herbs in any form until your health issues are resolved.

Now that the disclaimers are out of the way, you can delve into the different techniques for connecting with Hekate. As this will be your first time contacting and working with the goddess, the following approaches have a meditational format. Medication and mindfulness techniques are proven to improve focus. They'll teach you how to concentrate on your intention in future work. Below are a few approaches to bonding with Hekate and tips on making them work for you. Remember, working with the goddess of transformation is highly personal. While following the techniques below can be a sound way to start, they'll only have full effects if you make them your own.

Journeying to Meet Hekate

This meditation will help you meet and communicate with Hekate at her sacred crossroads. You'll stay in one place for 8-10 minutes, so make sure to find a comfortable position and support for your back if needed. Here is how to start the journey to meet Hekate:

1. Assume a comfortable position - preferably sitting cross-legged. Alternatively, you can lie down on a mat. Rest your hand on your legs and ensure your back is relaxed.
2. Take three deep breaths. When doing this, use your abdominal muscles. That way, your breathing becomes even deeper. Every time you inhale, exhale slowly with a long, audible sigh.
3. After the third exhale, examine your body to see if you're relaxed and comfortable or need to adjust your position.
4. Close your eyes and picture yourself walking along a dark, graveled path on a quiet night. Visualize a waning moon rising over the tree lines. You can only hear the sound of the night - crickets in nearby bushes and the call of an owl reaching you from a faraway tree.
5. Keep walking confidently forward in your vision, and try to enjoy the solitude and companionship of the sound the crunching

gravel makes beneath your feet. It's cold, and you can see the little puffs your breath makes in the chill of the late evening air.
6. As you walk, picture a flickering light up ahead of you. As you get closer, you'll see the light coming from a torch marking the crossroads. The closer you get, the more detailed the image becomes. You can see offerings left by other devotees at the signpost.
7. Next, visualize a small offering you're carrying in your hands. This could be a small bundle of homemade bread, an apple, or anything else that comes to mind.
8. As you reach the crossroads, the wind picks up, carrying a swirl of roads across the crossroads. Stop for a moment to take in the captivating scene. Approach the torchlight area as quietly as possible.
9. Take a deep breath and leave your offering while saying a quiet prayer to Hekate. As you do, start focusing on your surroundings. While you're perfectly comfortable being alone at night, you suddenly pick up a source of energy in the air.
10. As you try to figure out where the energy comes from, you suddenly hear howling dogs. The wind becomes even stronger, making you gasp as it swirls around you, and you battle to see what's happening. You feel the earth tremble beneath your feet and hear a deep rumbling noise. If you feel unstable, visualize yourself grabbing the signpost to keep yourself upright.
11. Now, picture the noise and the winds fading away and the night becoming silent and peaceful again. Your offering is now on the ground. However, as you turn slowly, you realize you're not alone.
12. Next, visualize a large black dog running to you and affectionately greeting you. Feel free to pet the dog and play with it, giving in to the laughter the free spirit of animals often brings out from people. As you're scratching the dog's ears, it suddenly signals that someone is approaching - a woman dressed in an elaborate black hooded cape.
13. As you see the woman approaching silently on her sandal-clad feet, an owl flies in and lands gracefully on the top of the signpost. It blinks its wide eyes at you and ruffles its feathers. Nervous, you prepare to greet the woman by bowing your head.

After greeting her, you look up to discover that she is a regal-looking middle-aged woman wearing a silver crown. However, as you continue looking at her, her face starts to change - first to a young woman, then to a much older one with white hair.

14. Focus on the woman's eyes - they're black and radiate with timeless wisdom. Visualize her greeting you and thanking you for visiting her in her sacred place. While she might look intimidating, try not to be afraid of her. This will prompt her to reassure you that she will not bring you death or misfortune. Instead, she will assist you through any changes upon you and escort you to the next stage of your life.

15. Picture her giving you tree keys as gifts. These represent knowledge, intuition, and magic. Hekate instructs you to hold these gifts close to your heart and not hesitate to call on her when you need her. Feel the warmth coursing through your body when you raise the keys to your heart and whisper your thanks.

16. Lastly, visualize Hekate turning away and slowly walking away from you, accompanied by her dog and owl. A mist seems to swallow them up as you let their image disappear from your view. The last image in your vision should be that of the signpost - should you ever wish to return there, it will be waiting for you.

17. Take a deep breath, grounding yourself again, and let the journey take you back home. As you find yourself back in your room, bring your attention back to your breath. Take three slow, audible breaths to bring yourself all the way back. Have a stretch, and when you feel ready, open your eyes and slowly return to your everyday activities.

Meditating on a Symbol

Meditation allows you to connect with Hekate.
https://unsplash.com/photos/V-TIPBoC_2M

One of the easiest ways to connect with Hekate is through one of her symbols. Draw it on a piece of paper and meditate with it to bring the goddess's energy closer to you. Here is how to do it:

1. Start by assuming a comfortable position in a quiet room at night. Make sure that you won't be disturbed for at least 10-15 minutes before you start your meditation.
2. Take the symbol of your hands and great the goddess:

   "Goddess Hekate, Queen of all Witches
   Host of the underworld and things unseen
   Custodian of crossroads and liminal places
   Queen of dead and transforming spaces
   The Soul of night animals and moonlight
   I greet you this night."
3. Visualize the symbol in front of your eyes (or keep looking at it on the paper - whichever helps you more).
4. Take a few breaths and focus on feeling a potent energy source emanating from the symbol.

5. Feel the goddess's energy reaching you, enveloping your body, carrying Hekate's gifts. Feel it empowering you, preparing you for your subsequent challenges, and lifting you up spiritually.
6. Continue focusing on the energy of the symbol until you feel prepared to complete your meditation.
7. When ready, let the image of the symbol with the energy fade away (and let the paper fall from your hands if you were holding it).
8. Exhale deeply, and let your mind return to your mundane thoughts.

Meditating in the Dark

This night-time meditation focuses on embracing the dark home of Hekate and inviting her into your world. As with any other meditation or mindfulness technique, you start by getting comfortable in a place where you won't be disturbed. For practical purposes, choosing a place near your altar where you can place a candle and light it for Hekate is recommended. Here is how to perform this mediation:

1. After lighting a candle, turning off all the lights, and assuming a comfortable position, take a deep breath.
2. As you exhale, let go of any tension you feel in your body and allow your mind to sink into a state of relaxedness and ease.
3. Focusing on the candle flame, let your everyday thoughts drift far away. Visualize them floating away until you can't see them with your mind's eye.
4. Take another slow deep breath and focus on feeling safe in the here and now as you prepare to travel into the deep night. There, you'll meet Hekate and reveal the deepest parts of yourself.
5. Picture yourself wrapped in a long cloak - feeling safe under the goddess's protection. As you look away from your black velvet cloak, you suddenly see yourself in a lush, green, earthy meadow at night. You start exploring the meadow as the sounds of the night accompany you.
6. Visualize an entrance in a tree nearby the meadow. As you approach the entrance, you'll see five stairs leading to a gate guarded by three black dogs. As you descend the steps, you start feeling the divine energy reaching out to you, making you more

confident in your purpose.

7. As you reach the entrance, tap into your mind, and look for painful memories you wish to leave behind. Acknowledging each one, offer these memories to the guardian dogs.
8. You'll feel lighter as you see the dogs burying your memories deep into the ground. The animals allow you to pass and meet Hekate.
9. Picture the goddess in front of you, dressed in the same black robe you are - the symbol of her energy residing within you. She offers her protection, and you accept it. Take in her picture and know that just as she survived many challenges, so will you until your soul's journey in this life is over.
10. Before you leave her side, offer the goddess a small token of gratitude as an offering. This could be a thought of worthlessness, prejudice, or any negative emotion you want to leave behind. Imagine Hekate placing these thoughts and feelings into a blue cauldron, where they disappear into the smoke of the magic she is brewing.
11. To fill the space left behind by the negative thoughts and emotions, Hekate offers you her blessings. Accept them and feel your body and mind relaxed and safe as they reach you.
12. As her energy seeps into your darkest secret, take three deep breaths and let the emotions that come with the secret break free. Embrace any emotions you feel - sadness, rage, anxiety, etc. - in the here and now.
13. Now imagine these feelings as rooms in your consciousness. As the magic from the goddess continues emanating towards your body and mind, they reach the dark rooms, swallowing the negative emotions and leaving nothing behind.
14. Continue reminiscing on the effects of the healing energy until you're ready to return. Then, take three slow, easy breaths and thank Hekate for her gifts and healing. Turn away from the goddess, and walk back up the stairs through the meadow, slowly bringing awareness back to the present.
15. Once you're ready, open your eyes and feel revitalized and filled with positive energy.

Reading the Orphic Hymn to Hekate

1. Reading the Orphic Hymn to Hekate (you'll find this in the bonus chapter) is another splendid way to express your intention of meeting them and working with them. Here is how to offer this hymn in a few simple steps:
2. Light a purple candle on your altar. Place offerings and symbols of the goddess around the candle. Keep the text of the hymn within your reach.
3. Get comfortable in front of the altar. Gaze into the candle and focus on relaxing your mind and body.
4. Take a few deep breaths, then start reading the hymn. Do it slowly, and when you reach the end, pause, and look into the candle flame again. Repeat this two more times.
5. By the time you're finished with the last repetition, night has fallen, and you're ready to go to bed. As you do, prepare for a restful sleep with the goddess's blessings.

Hekate Mediation at a Threshold

Meditating at a threshold is the easiest way to reach Hekate's sacred crossroads as a beginner. Make sure the threshold you're using is undisturbed so you can focus on the exercise without interruption. Here is how to meditate with Hekate at a threshold:

1. Start at dusk. This is a time of transition when the goddess's power is at its strongest. Turn off all the lights and electronic devices nearby, and sit near the threshold. Lean your back against something supporting it, and place a cushion behind it. You can also cover yourself with a cozy blanket, as it might get chilly.
2. Take a deep breath and close your eyes. When you're ready, picture yourself walking uphill toward a beautiful patch of nature. Despite the approaching darkness, you can see that the grass is vivid green, just like the crown of the trees.
3. You feel a light breeze and the scent of the woods as you easily stroll toward the trees. As you pass them, up ahead, you'll see light coming from beyond the trees. Imagine yourself walking towards the light and suddenly reaching the top of the hill, which

is also a cliff. Down below, you can see the dark ocean.
4. Instead of a steep pathway leading down the cliff, imagine a gently curving path leading to the ocean. Take this path, and feel yourself relaxing with each step.
5. When you reach the bottom of the hill, you feel sand under your feet. It's soft and gentle, and as you stroll along the beach, you hear the sound of the waves meeting the sand.
6. Further down the beach, you see a cave. Stroll towards it, and don't fear entering it. Take a few deep breaths if you need to calm yourself. Feel the soothing energy emanating from the cave as the goddess invites you into her home.
7. Picture yourself entering a brightly lit cave. As your eyes adjust to the lights, you'll see that the cave is much deeper than it seemed from the outside. From the cave's depths emerges a female figure and reaches what's revealed to be the crossroads.
8. See yourself smiling at Hekate as she smiles back at you and embraces you with her nurturing energy. As you start your journey together, you can ask the goddess what she wants you to know today. If you aren't prepared to ask her anything, you can just stand here, letting her presence relax and empower you.
9. Let the image of Hekate disappear, but you can remain at the crossroads as long as you want to. You can even let yourself drift off to sleep if you wish.
10. When you're ready, leave the cave. As you step outside, let the sounds of the ocean bring you back to reality. Stretch yourself and open your eyes when you feel ready.

Meeting the Goddess

This is another method for meeting the goddess. It's similar to journeying but a much more straightforward process. However, it requires plenty of concentration. Here is how to do it:
1. Prepare for going to bed. Besides preparing yourself, make sure that your bedroom is as soothing a place as possible, suitable for a relaxing practice and sleep afterward. Avoid using electronics for at least an hour before going to bed. This way, your mind can slowly unwind and focus on the exercise.

2. When you're ready, turn off the lights and lie down. Feel comfortable and close your eyes.
3. Take a few deep breaths until you feel your mind and body relaxing.
4. Visualize yourself walking down a dark tunnel slowly while calling on the goddess. See her appear before you at the other end of the tunnel.
5. Say a few words of greeting and gratitude for their presence.
6. Slowly let the vision fade away, take a deep breath, and let yourself fall asleep naturally.

Chapter 5: Hekatean Herblore

In Greek mythology, the goddess Hekate was revered as the queen of witches and the guardian of the crossroads. Her power was said to extend beyond the physical realm and into the spiritual, where she was known to guide and protect those who asked for her help. However, the most significant aspect of Hekate's domain was her connection to herbs and their mystical properties. According to legends, Hekate was an expert in herbal knowledge and created various herbal concoctions that could bring about extraordinary changes in the natural world. These herbal infusions were said to be filled with Hekate's sacred energy, which could be used to heal or harm, depending on the practitioner's intentions. The herbs associated with Hekate hold the key to unlocking and manifesting the witch goddess's potent magic. For instance, Mugwort, a favorite herb of the goddess, was often burned as incense during rituals and rites to call upon her powers.

People who sought Hekate's guidance and help in matters of the heart and spirit often turned to herbs associated with her to communicate with the goddess. It was believed that certain plants, such as mandrake or datura, could open a channel of communication between the physical and spiritual realms, allowing one to connect with the goddess directly. In this chapter, you will explore the many herbs associated with Hekate and the intricate web of myth and magic surrounding them. From their historical uses to their use in modern Wiccan rituals, you will delve into the world of herblore and discover the secrets of Hekate's mystical garden.

Herbs Associated with Hekate

The herbs associated with Hekate are as diverse as they are potent. Each one is said to hold a unique connection to the goddess and her power, making them a crucial part of any practitioner's toolkit. These include:

1. Yew

Yew is a tree with a long history of being associated with magic and mysticism. Due to its potent properties and symbolic significance, many cultures have considered it sacred. In Wiccan and Hekatean cultures, yew is a particularly powerful plant that has a special connection to the goddess, Hekate. The yew tree symbolizes death and the underworld. In Greek mythology, it was believed that the yew was sacred to Hekate because it grew near the entrance to the underworld. The tree was seen as a portal between the physical and spiritual realms and was considered a conduit for communicating with the goddess. Historically, yew has been used in various cultures as a means of divination and protection. Druids in ancient Britain considered the yew to be a sacred tree and used its branches in their magical practices. The ancient Celts also believed it had the power to protect against evil spirits and curses.

The yew tree has been associated with mysticism.
https://pixabay.com/es/photos/tejo-tejo-ingl%c3%a9s-frutos-rojos-6678612/

In modern times, yew is still used in various forms of spellwork and ritual. One popular way to use yew is to create an incense blend that can be burned during ceremonies to honor Hekate or to call upon her power. To make a yew incense blend, combine dried yew leaves with other herbs and resins associated with the goddess, such as mugwort, frankincense, and myrrh. Another way to incorporate yew into your magical practice is to create a protection pouch. To do this, carve a small piece of yew wood into a shape representing Hekate or one of her symbols, such as a key or a torch. Place the carved wood in a small pouch along with other protective herbs and crystals, such as black tourmaline or sage. This pouch can be carried with you or placed in a specific area of your home to create a protective barrier.

2. Cypress

The cypress tree is one of the most enigmatic and intriguing trees in the natural world. It stands tall and imposing, starkly contrasting with the gentle, weeping willows that sway in the breeze. For centuries, the cypress has been linked to the goddess Hekate, and its symbolism and mythology make it a powerful addition to any magical practice. This tree is often associated with the concept of transformation, particularly regarding Hekate's herblore. In Greek mythology, it was believed that Hekate was the goddess of transitions - the guide and protector of souls as they moved from one world to the next. With its tall, dark silhouette, the cypress was seen as a symbol of this journey, with the tree's roots reaching down into the underworld.

The Cypress tree is associated with transformation.
https://pixabay.com/es/photos/cipreses-toscana-paisaje-avenida-3701931/

The cypress is a tree that has long been linked to the concept of purification. In ancient times, people would burn the tree's wood and needles to cleanse their homes and protect themselves from negative energy. Today, cypress essential oil is still used in many spiritual and magical practices to purify and cleanse the environment. This oil can be added to bathwater, diffused in a room, or used in a homemade cleansing spray. The cypress is also said to have protective properties, making it a popular ingredient in many spells and rituals. Its energy is considered especially powerful regarding matters of the heart and relationships. Some practitioners use its oil to create a protective charm for a loved one or to promote self-love and healing.

If you want to incorporate cypress into your magical practice, there are many ways to do so. You can create an altar dedicated to Hekate and adorn it with cypress branches, cones, and candles. You can also use its wood to create a wand or staff that you can use to channel the goddess's transformative energy. For a more subtle touch, simply carry a piece of cypress wood in your pocket to keep the goddess's energy close to you throughout the day.

3. Witch Hazel

Witch hazel, also known as winter bloom, is a flowering shrub that is associated with the goddess Hekate in her role as a healer and protector. Witch hazel has long been used in traditional medicine for its anti-inflammatory, astringent, and soothing properties, making it a powerful addition to any magical practice. Hekate's association with witch hazel is linked to its healing properties and ability to cleanse and purify. Ancient magic practitioners often called upon the goddess to help heal the sick and injured, and witch hazel was used in many of these healing rituals. Its astringent properties were used to treat skin conditions, while its anti-inflammatory properties were used to reduce swelling and pain.

Witch hazel cleanses and purifies.

Si Griffiths, CC BY-SA 3.0 DEED < https://creativecommons.org/licenses/by-sa/3.0/deed.en>, via Wikimedia Commons https://commons.wikimedia.org/wiki/File:Witch-hazel_(Hamamelis)_In_Flower,_RHS_Wisley_Garden_Surrey_UK.jpg

In Hekate's herblore, witch hazel is also associated with protection and banishing negative energy. Its cleansing properties are said to purify spaces and remove any unwanted energy or spirits. The shrub's branches and leaves can create a protective barrier or ward off evil spirits around the home. If you wish to incorporate witch hazel into your magical practice, there are many ways to do so. You can create a witch hazel infusion for healing spells or to cleanse and purify your home.

You can also use the shrub's leaves and branches in a protection spell or charm, carrying it with you to ward off negative energy and protect you from harm. You can create a witch hazel-based spray for banishing spells by mixing witch hazel extract with essential oils known for their banishing properties, such as sage, cedarwood, or rosemary. Simply spray the mixture around your home or on your person to banish negative energy and spirits.

4. Black Poplar

The black poplar, also known as Populus nigra, is a species of tree strongly associated with Hekate, the Greek goddess of witchcraft, magic, and the night. The tree's connection to the goddess can be traced back to ancient times when it was believed that the rustling of the leaves was the voice of the goddess herself. Black poplar is associated with transformation, renewal, and the mysteries of death and rebirth. The tree's tall and slender stature, with its roots planted firmly in the underworld, symbolizes the goddess's connection to the spiritual world and the mysteries of the afterlife. The black poplar was also believed to be a source of divination, as its leaves and branches were used to make oracular pronouncements.

Black poplar is used for transformation and renewal.
David Hawgood / Black Poplar, near Milton Common, CC BY-SA 2.0 DEED <https://creativecommons.org/licenses/by-sa/2.0/deed.en> via Wikimedia Commons https://commons.wikimedia.org/wiki/File:Black_Poplar,_near_Milton_Common_-_geograph.org.uk_-_245091.jpg

Historically, the black poplar was used in a variety of magical rituals and spells, particularly those related to transformation and renewal. Its bark and leaves were used to make teas, tinctures, and poultices to aid in healing and help with life transitions, such as birth, death, and spiritual awakening. The tree's wood was also used to create wands, believed to help the practitioner connect with the energies of transformation and change. Today, black poplar is still used in magical practices to aid in transformation and renewal. Its leaves can be dried and burned as incense to help with meditation and connect with the goddess's transformative energy. The bark and leaves can also be used to create tea, which can be consumed to aid in spiritual healing and help with transitions in life.

5. Garlic

With its potent aroma and powerful properties, garlic has long been associated with Hekate. In Hekate's herblore, garlic is known as a protective herb that can banish negativity and evil spirits. In ancient times, garlic was believed to be a potent weapon against dark forces and malevolent spirits. Its strong scent was thought to be harmful to evil beings and that it could drive them away. For this reason, it was often placed at the entrance to homes or hung in windows to ward off negative energies.

Garlic is used to keep dark forces and spirits away.
https://unsplash.com/photos/yIiye0QDryo

In Hekate's magic, garlic is used to protect the practitioner from harm and to banish negative energy. Its pungent scent is said to clear the air of negativity and create a protective barrier around the practitioner. It can be used in a variety of magical workings, from creating protective charms to adding it to food for its magical properties. Today, garlic is still a powerful tool in modern magical practices. It can be used to create protective sachets or amulets, added to cleansing baths, or burned as incense to create a protective atmosphere. It can also be used in culinary magic, where its flavor and magical properties can be incorporated into recipes to promote healing and protection.

6. Lavender

Lavender, with its soft purple hues and delicate fragrance, is a beloved herb in the world of magic and folklore. It is said to have been associated with Hekate, the Greek goddess of witchcraft, for its calming properties and ability to soothe the mind and spirit. In Hekate's herblore, lavender is often used in spells and rituals to promote peace, harmony, and balance. Its gentle energy is said to align the chakras and calm the mind, making it a powerful tool for meditation and divination. Lavender's association with Hekate is also tied to its connection to the moon. Hekate is often depicted as a lunar goddess, and lavender is believed to be ruled by the moon. The herb's delicate purple flowers are said to represent the moon's gentle glow, while its calming properties mirror the moon's soothing energy.

Lavender is used to calm and soothe the mind.
https://unsplash.com/photos/ClWvcrkBhMY

In addition to its magical properties, lavender is a popular herb in aromatherapy and herbal medicine. Its soothing fragrance is believed to have a calming effect on the nervous system, making it a popular remedy for anxiety, stress, and insomnia. To incorporate lavender into your magical practice, you can use it in various ways, from creating herbal sachets to burning lavender-scented candles. You can also add lavender to your bathwater to promote relaxation and create a sense of inner peace.

7. Myrrh

Myrrh, with its spicy, resinous scent and ancient history, is a powerful herb in the world of magic and mythology. In ancient times, it was highly valued for its healing properties and used as a currency in some cultures. Myrrh is associated with the underworld and the afterlife in Hekate's herb lore. Its use in funerary rites dates back to ancient times, and it was often burned as an offering to the gods. As the goddess of witchcraft and the keeper of the keys to the underworld, Hekate is often invoked in rituals involving myrrh.

Myrrh has powerful healing properties.
https://pixabay.com/es/photos/mirra-natividad-navidad-jes%c3%bas-6050657/

The symbolism of myrrh is also tied to its powerful healing properties. It is often used to banish negative energies and to purify the mind, body, and spirit. It promotes healing, boosts the immune system, and calms the nerves. Myrrh is a versatile herb that can be used in various ways in your magical practice; you can burn it as incense to banish negative energies and to create a protective barrier around yourself or your home. You can add it to an herbal bath to promote healing and purification.

8. Mugwort

Mugwort is deeply tied to the world of magic and spirituality. It has long been used in many cultures for its powerful properties and is often associated with the goddess Hekate. In Hekate's herblore, mugwort is seen as a herb of protection, especially for women and travelers. It enhances psychic abilities and opens the third eye, making it a popular herb for divination and lucid dreaming. It is also used to aid in astral projection and enhance intuition.

Mugwort is often used for lunar rituals.
AnemoneProjectors, CC BY-SA 2.0 <https://creativecommons.org/licenses/by-sa/2.0>, via Wikimedia Commons
https://commons.wikimedia.org/wiki/File:Mugwort_(Artemisia_vulgaris)_(24244929842).jpg

Symbolically, mugwort is associated with the moon and the element of air. Its silvery leaves and soft, feathery texture evoke the moon's energy and make it a popular herb for lunar rituals. In addition, its light and airy quality makes it useful for spells and rituals that involve movement and transformation. Mugwort is a versatile herb that can be used in various ways in your magical practice. You can burn mugwort as incense to enhance your psychic abilities and aid in divination. You can add it to a dream pillow to encourage lucid dreaming or drink it as a tea to aid astral projection.

9. Cardamom

In Hekate's herblore, cardamom is seen as a herb of transformation and protection. It is said to have the power to dispel negative energy and attract positive energy. As a spice highly valued in ancient times, cardamom has a long history of use in various forms of magic, including incense and spells. It was a popular herb in ancient Egyptian and Greek magic and Ayurvedic medicine. It was believed to have healing properties and was used to treat various ailments, including digestive issues and respiratory problems. It was also used as an aphrodisiac and was thought to increase sexual potency.

Cardamom attracts positive energy.
https://unsplash.com/photos/2P0EFD18NYA

In modern magic, cardamom is often used in spells and rituals related to protection, purification, and transformation. It is said to have the power to dispel negative energy and attract positive energy, making it a valuable tool for spiritual practitioners. It can be burned as incense or added to bath water to purify and cleanse the body and mind.

10. Mint

In Hekate's herblore, mint is considered a powerful herb of the moon and is often associated with the goddess's association with the underworld. It is believed to help one connect with their intuitive and psychic abilities and is often used in divination and spiritual exploration rituals. Mint has a long history of use in traditional medicine and magic. It was used by the ancient Greeks and Romans to treat various ailments, including digestive issues, headaches, and respiratory problems. It was also used to freshen breath and flavor food.

Mint is used for rituals and spells for divination and intuition.
https://www.pexels.com/photo/green-mint-photo-214165/

In magic, mint is often used in spells and rituals related to divination, intuition, and spiritual exploration. It is believed to have the power to connect one with the spiritual realm, making it a valuable tool for spiritual practitioners. It can be burned as incense or used in spells to open up one's intuitive abilities and enhance psychic awareness. It is also associated with the element of air, believed to represent the power of communication and intellect. This association with air makes mint a valuable tool for those seeking to improve their communication skills or connect more deeply with the spiritual realm.

11. Dandelion

Dandelion is often associated with the Greek goddess Hekate and has been used in her herblore for centuries. The plant is revered for its association with the underworld and its ability to help one connect with their inner power and strength. The bright yellow flowers of the dandelion are believed to represent the power of the sun, while the white, fluffy seeds represent the power of the wind. This combination of solar and lunar energy makes dandelions a powerful tool for transformation and growth, a key aspect of Hekate's association with magic.

Dandelions represent the power of the sun.
Greg Hume, CC BY-SA 3.0 <https://creativecommons.org/licenses/by-sa/3.0>, via Wikimedia Commons https://commons.wikimedia.org/wiki/File:DandelionFlower.jpg

In ancient times, dandelion was used as a medicinal herb to treat a variety of ailments, including liver problems, digestive issues, and skin conditions. It was also used in divination rituals to help practitioners connect with the spiritual realm and gain insight into their future. In Hekate's herblore, dandelion is often used to enhance intuition, increase psychic abilities, and encourage personal growth and transformation. The herb is believed to help one eliminate old patterns and habits, allowing a more authentic and empowered self to emerge. It is also used in protection spells and rituals, as its association with the underworld and the sun offers powerful protection against negative energies and entities. It can be burned as incense, added to spell bags or sachets, or used in spiritual baths to promote purification and protection.

12. Hellebore

Hellebore has long been associated with the Greek goddess Hekate and her magic. It is said to possess powerful energies that can be used to bring about transformation, protection, and connection to the spiritual realm. The hellebore plant has been used in medicinal remedies for thousands of years and was considered a cure for many ailments, including madness, melancholy, and fever. However, its use in magical practices is where its association with Hekate comes in.

Hellebore is used for its protective qualities.
https://pixabay.com/es/photos/helleborus-niger-rosa-de-navidad-7029641/

In Hekate's herblore, hellebore is often used for its protective qualities. It is believed to ward off negative energies, entities, and spirits, making it an important ingredient in spells and rituals of banishing and protection. It is also associated with transformation and rebirth and is used in spells and rituals to help individuals release old patterns and embrace new beginnings. It is a powerful tool for those seeking to connect with the spiritual realm and the wisdom of the goddess.

In addition to its protective and transformative properties, hellebore is associated with divination and prophecy. It enhances one's intuition and psychic abilities, making it an ideal herb for those seeking to develop their spiritual gifts. However, it is important to note that hellebore is poisonous and should not be ingested fresh. It should only be used in its dried form or as an infusion in spiritual baths or washes.

These powerful plants have long been used to connect with the transformative energy of the goddess of the crossroads. From the potent protection of yew to the cleansing and purifying energy of hellebore, each one has its own unique symbolism and magic. When working with these herbs, it is important to honor their power and approach them with respect and intention. Whether you choose to create an incense blend, brew an infusion, or craft a protection pouch, the herbs associated with Hekate offer a powerful tool for connecting with the wisdom and magic of this ancient goddess. As you explore the world of Hekate's herblore, remember that this is just the beginning of a deep and transformative journey. By incorporating these herbs into your magical practice, you can connect with the goddess's energy, embrace your inner power, and unlock the full potential of your spiritual journey.

Chapter 6: Creating an Altar for Hekate

Crafting an altar for Hekate is a profoundly intimate and spiritual encounter that is vital to any Hekatean ritual. An altar serves as a hallowed sanctuary where you can establish a profound bond with Hekate, pay homage to her, and seek her wisdom. Whether you are new to the realm of Modern Hekatean Witchcraft or a seasoned practitioner, crafting an altar dedicated to Hekate offers an exceptional opportunity to enrich your practice and form a closer connection with the Witchcraft Goddess.

Hekate is a powerful and enigmatic goddess known for her association with magic, witchcraft, crossroads, and liminality. As the mother of witchcraft, she is a guiding force for witches and magical practitioners worldwide. Creating an altar dedicated to her is a way to show your respect and devotion to this powerful deity. An altar for Hekate is not just a tool for witchcraft; it's also a place of power and transformation. It's a sacred space where you can communicate with the divine, seek guidance, and explore your spirituality. Whether you're seeking answers to life's big questions or working on manifesting your desires, an altar for Hekate can be an invaluable tool on your journey.

In this chapter, you'll explore the elements of creating an altar for Hekate, including the tools and symbols that are commonly used in Modern Hekatean Witchcraft. It'll also delve into the specifics of setting up your altar, including how to arrange your tools and offerings to reflect your personal witchcraft and devotion to the goddess. By the end of this chapter, you'll have all the knowledge and inspiration you need to create a personalized and powerful altar dedicated to the goddess of witches. It's time to connect with Hekate and let her guide you on your spiritual journey.

Altar vs. Shrine

An altar is a space reserved for showcasing religious artifacts that hold significant meaning. The term "altar" is derived from "alter," which means to change. In Wicca, an altar may hold tools to practice their faith, such as an athame, deity representations, and items symbolizing the four elements or directions.

Nonetheless, the use of "altar" to describe a sanctified space displaying objects of worship for Hekate has been a matter of contention among her followers and practitioners of Hekatean witchcraft. Some argue that the appropriate term for this arrangement is a shrine, not an altar. If you intend to express devotion to Hekate, it's best to use the term *shrine* instead of *altar*. You can choose to merge both a shrine and an altar into a single sacred location if that resonates with you. Ultimately, it's your decision to determine the language that best suits your practice and feels right for you.

A shrine is a sacred space dedicated to expressing devotion and worship to a deity or spirit. It is a place where offerings are left, and prayers are said, a focal point for the expression of one's spiritual relationship with a particular being. In the case of Hekate, the goddess of witches, it is common for devotees to have a shrine in her honor. Shrines to Hekate often include images or representations of her and offerings such as candles, incense, and food. Keys are a common symbol associated with Hekate, representing her ability to unlock mysteries and open doors. Many devotees include keys on their shrines to express gratitude for Hekate's assistance in their lives.

Shrines can also serve as a place to petition Hekate for assistance or guidance. This can include placing offerings or items on the shrine that are infused with a specific intention or request, such as a photo of a loved one needing help. While a shrine is primarily a place of devotion and worship, it can also be used for divination practices. Many devotees use their shrines to communicate with the dead or receive messages from the goddess. Ultimately, the objects and offerings that one includes on their shrine should reflect their personal relationship with the goddess and their unique witchcraft practice. While common symbols and items are associated with Hekate, such as keys and portrayals of her, it is ultimately up to the individual to determine what they wish to include.

Setting Up the Altar

When creating a shrine to honor Hekate, consider including a representation of her, such as a statue or picture. Many beautiful works of art are available, and if you choose to use artwork, make sure to buy a copy instead of just downloading and printing it. If you don't have the budget, look for public-domain images. Hekate, being the Queen of the Witches, appreciates having her own altar or altar space in a witch's home. In addition, you can also add items such as a cauldron, a knife, a broom, dog figurines, and decorations with stars and moons. It's important to cleanse and consecrate the space and tools in Hekate's name before setting them up, and then re-cleanse and charge them monthly on the Dark Moon. Remember that your shrine may start simple but will grow with time. Here are some guidelines you can keep in mind when setting up an altar for Hekate.

1. **Choosing The Location**

Choosing the right location for your altar is crucial to setting up a sacred space for Hekate. When deciding where to place your altar, consider factors such as privacy, accessibility, and atmosphere. You can choose a corner of your bedroom, a space on a bookshelf, or a small table in a quiet area of your home. The location you choose should be a place where you feel comfortable and safe, a place where you can focus your intention and energy.

When you're picking a spot, think about the energy of the space. Is it a place where you feel connected to nature or a place that feels dark and mysterious? Perhaps it's a space with a view of the night sky or a window that lets in natural light. Once you've chosen your spot, it's important to cleanse and consecrate it. You might use smoke from burning sage or incense to purify the space or sprinkle salt water to cleanse it. As you do that, call on Hekate to bless the area and protect it from negative energy.

2. **When to Set It Up**

When creating an altar for Hekate, timing can play an important role in building a stronger connection with this goddess. It's recommended to create the altar when the moon's energy is at its peak, such as on the night of the full moon, the new moon, or on a Monday. Here's why:

Firstly, the full moon is a time of heightened energy, abundance, and manifestation. It's a time when the moon is fully illuminated and radiating with powerful energy. Creating an altar for Hekate during the full moon can amplify your intentions and strengthen your bond with her, as the moon's energy will support your efforts. On the other hand, the new moon represents a time of new beginnings and fresh starts. It's a time for setting intentions and planting seeds for the future. By creating an altar for Hekate during the new moon, you'll tap into this energy and invite her to help you on your new journey.

Mondays are also a great time to create an altar for Hekate, as this day is associated with the moon and the goddess. Mondays are considered the best day for working with Hekate, as they provide an opportunity to start the week strong and focused. Creating an altar during these peak moon times can ensure that your intentions align with the moon's phases. This can provide a greater sense of harmony and balance in your life, which is key for any spiritual practice.

3. Keeping It Personal

When it comes to setting up a shrine to Hekate, it's important to keep it personal. While you can certainly purchase items to add to your shrine, creating your own objects can be one of the most meaningful ways to express devotion to Hekate. Don't worry if you don't consider yourself artistically inclined. The love and intention you put into the object matters most, not how great it looks on social media. However, if you're not inclined to create your own objects, that's perfectly fine too. What's important is that the objects you choose for your shrine are personal and reflect your feelings about Hekate.

Note that unlike in some Pagan traditions, Hekate does not reside in objects. Therefore, attempting to put her into an object is inappropriate. This would be considered blasphemy. Hekate is a powerful and multifaceted goddess who exists independently of any physical object. Therefore, when choosing objects for your shrine, it's important to remember that they are simply symbols of your relationship with her. Ultimately, the key to creating a personal shrine to Hekate is to let your intuition guide you. Choose objects that resonate with you and that you feel drawn to. Doing so will create a space uniquely your own and reflect the deep connection you share with this powerful and ancient goddess.

4. Hekate Colors

Hekate is often associated with specific colors that can be incorporated into her shrine. The colors most commonly associated with her are black, red, and white. These colors can be used in a variety of ways, from candles to fabric to cutouts made from paper. Black, in particular, is a color strongly associated with Hekate and can be used to represent the night, the unknown, and the mysteries of the underworld. Red is another color that is associated with Hekate, and it can be used to represent her power and passion. It can be used in candles, fabric, or other decorative items you may choose to include in your shrine. White, on the other hand, can be used to represent purity and clarity. It can be used as a background color for your shrine or as an accent color for decorative items.

Another color associated with Hekate is yellow or saffron. This color represents the harvest and the bountiful gifts of the earth. It can be used in fabric or in the form of decorative items like flowers or fruit. In addition to these colors, you may also want to consider the colors of objects associated with Hekate. For example, green is the color of oak trees, which are sacred to Hekate. You may want to include green in your shrine to represent the natural world and the power of the earth. Overall, using colors associated with Hekate is a great way to add depth and meaning to your shrine. By incorporating these colors in candles, fabric, or other decorative items, you can create a unique and personal space for your devotion to this powerful goddess.

5. Offerings

When it comes to offerings for a Hekate shrine, many traditional objects have been associated with Her throughout history. These can include things like garlic, saffron, oak leaves, and certain types of food. However, it's also important to consider personal objects that are significant to your devotion. For example, if you associate a particular flower with Hekate, you could include that in your shrine as an offering. Wild roses, which are associated with Hekate, are a great option for this. You can use them as permanent parts of the shrine or as offerings during the new moon phase. In addition to objects, you can also use symbols like dogs or snakes in your shrine. For example, having a statue of a dog or a snakeskin can be a great way to incorporate these symbols into your space.

Finally, it's worth noting that personal objects with symbolic meaning can be a powerful way to make offerings to Hekate. For example, you might include a piece of jewelry passed down to you by a family member or a small trinket that reminds you of a meaningful experience in your life. Whatever you choose, remember that the offering is meant to signify your devotion and appreciation for Hekate, so choose something that holds personal meaning for you.

6. Magical Tools and Sacred Objects

As a Modern Hekatean Witch, many sacred tools and magical objects can be used on your altar. These tools can help you connect with the energy of Hekate and aid in your magical workings. One of the most important things to keep in mind when choosing your tools is that they should be personal to you. You may want to consider making your own tools, as this can be a very meaningful way to express your devotion to Hekate.

Some examples of sacred tools that can be used on an altar include:

1. Knives and Blades

A knife is a common tool used in many magical traditions. It can be used for cutting herbs, carving symbols, and other practical purposes. Some witches use knives as offerings to Hekate, while others may use them for protection spells. As a Goddess associated with witchcraft and magic, Hekate is often linked to the use of knives and blades in rituals and spellwork. In Hecatean practice, knives and blades are considered sacred tools and are used to cut energy, cords, and other materials in spellwork.

Knives and blades are used for cutting cords, directing energy, and casting circles.
Matus Kalisky, CC BY-NC-ND 2.0 DEED < https://creativecommons.org/licenses/by-nc-nd/2.0/>, https://www.flickr.com/photos/31007239@N06/21477266240

The athame, a double-edged knife, is common in Wiccan and Hekatean practice. It is used for casting circles, directing energy, and cutting cords. The athame is traditionally black-handled, symbolizing the element of fire, which represents will, passion, and transformation. To consecrate an athame for use in Hekatean practice, it can be cleansed with salt water, smudged with herbs like sage or mugwort, and charged under the full moon's light or in the presence of Hekate's image or statue.

Swords are also sometimes used in Hecatean practice, as they are associated with strength, protection, and the ability to cut through obstacles. They can be used to cast a circle or to symbolically cut ties with negative influences or situations. To consecrate a sword for Hecatean practice, it can be cleansed with salt water, smudged with herbs like frankincense or myrrh, and charged in the presence of Hekate's image or statue.

2. Candles

Candles are essential to many spiritual and magical practices, including Hekatean witchcraft. They can be used to represent the element of fire, which is associated with transformation, passion, and energy. In Hecatean altars, candles are often used to honor the goddess and bring the practitioner light and clarity.

Candles are used to connect with Hekate.
https://pixabay.com/es/photos/vela-la-magia-ritual-magia-4702150/

Hekate is often associated with fire, as she is considered a goddess of transformation and illumination. Candles are a great way to connect with Hekate and create a sacred atmosphere in her honor. They can be used in various ways, such as during meditation, ritual, or spell work. When choosing candles for a Hekatean altar, it is recommended to use black or red candles, colors associated with the goddess. You can also use white candles, which represent purity and clarity. You can use other colors, depending on the intention of the ritual or spell, such as green for abundance or blue for healing.

Before using the candles, consecrate them to Hekate. This can be done by holding the candle in your hands and focusing your intention on the goddess. You can also anoint the candle with oils, such as frankincense or myrrh, associated with Hekate. Once the candle is consecrated, it is ready to be used in ritual or spell work. When lighting the candles, saying a prayer or invocation to Hekate is customary. This can be as simple as calling out her name or reciting a longer invocation. The candles should be allowed to burn completely and should never be left unattended. As the candles burn, they serve as a reminder of the presence of Hekate and the power of transformation and illumination she brings.

3. Keys

In Hecatean practice, keys are a common sacred tool as they symbolize Hekate's role as the goddess of liminality and as the keyholder to the mysteries. Keys can be purchased or handmade and are typically displayed on the altar. They can be made of metal, wood, or other materials. To consecrate a key for use in a Hekatean altar, start by cleansing it with water, salt, or incense to remove any negative energies. Then, hold the key in your hands and visualize it being filled with Hekate's energy and power. You can also choose to say a prayer or invocation to Hekate, asking for her blessing and protection over the key.

Keys are used as a symbol to unlock the mysteries of the universe.
https://www.pexels.com/photo/two-black-skeleton-keys-on-an-old-paper-612800/

Keys can be used in various rituals and spells. For example, a key can open or close a ritual circle, symbolically unlock the mysteries of the universe, or invoke Hekate's guidance and protection. They can also be used in divination practices, such as scrying or tarot readings, as a symbol for unlocking hidden knowledge or secrets. When using a key in a ritual or spell, it is important to focus on its intention and ask for Hekate's guidance and blessings. After the ritual or spell is complete, the key should be returned to the altar and kept safely until its next use.

In addition to these traditional tools, many Modern Hekatean witches use talismans, knot spells, and other creative methods in their magical workings. These can include using cords, charms, markers, and paints to create personalized spells and offerings. The possibilities are endless, and your tools should be unique to your own practice and personal connection with Hekate.

Creating an altar for Hekate can be a deeply personal and rewarding practice. Remember that your altar reflects your devotion and commitment to Hekate, and it can evolve and change over time as you deepen your relationship with her. Don't be afraid to experiment and try new things, and always trust your intuition when designing your altar. Whether you're just starting out on your spiritual journey or you're a seasoned practitioner, building an altar for Hekate can be a powerful way to deepen your connection with the divine and access the transformative power of magic. So, go forth, gather your tools, and start creating a sacred space that honors the wisdom and magic of Hekate!

Chapter 7: The Deipnon and Other Rituals

Ancient Greek magic was deeply intertwined with their religious beliefs, and their rituals and traditions were essential components of their daily lives. The Greeks believed in the existence of various gods and goddesses who were responsible for the different aspects of life. They believed these deities had the power to influence their lives, so they sought to appease them through various rituals and offerings.

One of the most important rituals in Ancient Greek magic was the Deipnon, held every month on the evening of the new moon. The Deipnon was a way for the Greeks to honor the goddess Hekate, the ruler of the underworld and the goddess of witchcraft, magic, and crossroads. The Greeks believed that Hekate had the power to grant them favors, protect them from evil spirits, and guide them through the dark of night.

During the Deipnon, offerings were made to Hekate and other gods and goddesses, including Zeus, Apollo, and Hermes. The offerings included libations, cakes, and incense, which were then left outside or on an altar. The Greeks believed that by making these offerings, they would gain the favor of the gods and receive their blessings.

The Deipnon was just one of many rituals that were an essential part of the Greek religious calendar. The Greeks celebrated various festivals and observances throughout the year, many linked to the seasons and the agricultural cycle. For example, Noumenia was a monthly observance held on the first day of the new moon, and it was a way for the Greeks to honor the god Apollo and ask for his blessings.

Another important ritual was the Home Blessing, performed annually to purify the home and ward off evil spirits. The Greeks believed that by performing this ritual, they would ensure the safety and prosperity of their household.

The Crossroads ritual was also an essential part of Ancient Greek magic. The Greeks believed that the crossroads were a place where the physical and spiritual worlds intersected; therefore, it was a place of great power. The Crossroads ritual was performed to invoke the aid of Hekate and other deities in matters related to magic and divination.

Ancient Greek magic was rich in ritualistic traditions and superstitions, and the Deipnon was just one of many important rituals performed to honor the gods and seek their favor. These rituals and beliefs were deeply intertwined with the Greek religious calendar and essential to their daily lives.

Hekate Rituals

Hekate's protection rituals are steeped in mysticism and ancient religious practices, and though the specifics may have changed over time, the core remains the same. Hekate's protection rituals are designed to keep away evil and negative energies while inviting positive energy and blessings into your life. These rituals often involve burning incense, invoking the goddess's presence, and making offerings to her. While some of these rituals can be complex and require a great deal of preparation, others are relatively simple and straightforward. Regardless of the complexity of the ritual, Hekate's protection rituals offer a powerful way to protect yourself, your home, and your loved ones. They keep away negative energies while inviting positive energy and blessings into your life. In addition, honoring or calling on Hekate involves meditative qualities that bring peace and harmony and create a sense of safety and security. The rituals can even protect you from harm and give you the strength to face life's challenges. They can also create a more harmonious and peaceful atmosphere in your home and your relationships.

Hekate's Deipnon

Hekate's Deipnon ritual is a mysterious and powerful ceremony shrouded in myth and speculation. Although the exact details of the ceremony remain unknown, what is known is that it was a monthly offering to Hekate, made on the night of the new moon. It has been linked to many different spiritual and magical practices. While the exact details of the ritual are still largely unknown, scholars have been able to piece together some symbols and meanings associated with it. Most of the ritual pertains to offerings and prayers intended to honor the goddess and placate her anger. It is a practice still carried out today by devotees who seek to unlock the mysteries of this ancient ritual and gain access to Hekate's power and protection.

Historical Practices

The ritual was performed at a crossroads, as these were believed sacred to Hekate and represented the point between the physical and spiritual worlds. Other locations included an altar or where air, water, and land met, such as on a bridge or a jutting rock. The ritual takes place on the darkest night of the year, usually around the end of the lunar month, which is thought to be a time of renewal and rebirth, and involves offerings of food and drink to the goddess. Participants in the ritual typically lit a candle and offered prayers and gifts to Hekate. The ritual was performed either as a solitary practice or with a group of like-minded individuals and was often accompanied by divination, with the purpose of seeking divine guidance and protection. It was believed to bring good luck and protection to the participant and their household. The ritual has three distinct parts.

- The first part was a meal consisting of food for the family and as an offering. Usually performed at a crossroads to honor the goddess and to thank her for her protection and guidance
- The second part of the ritual was the Expiation. This involved an animal sacrifice, such as a goat or a dog, to summon Hekate's benevolence
- The third part of the ritual was purification, which was performed to cleanse the home and ward off negative energies. This was typically carried out by burning incense, chanting prayers, and sprinkling holy water

The meal was the focal point of the ritual, with a variety of dishes such as fruits, vegetables, and grains being offered as a sign of respect. The family would take a few bites and offer the rest to the gods as a sign of respect. A typical Deipnon meal usually consisted of offerings of fish, honey, and sesame placed on the house's hearth. The meal was also shared with those who were not part of the family, including beggars and the poor, to commemorate the goddess' generosity.

All three portions of this ritual were an important part of honoring the goddess and receiving her blessings and was a time for reflection and contemplation. A time to reflect on one's spiritual journey and to ask for guidance and insight from Hekate. It was also an opportunity to let go of any pain, suffering, or negative emotions and commit to living a life of integrity and spiritual growth.

Modern Day Practices

Nowadays, the Deipnon ritual is often practiced as a way to remember and honor family members who have passed away. People will gather with family and friends to share memories and stories of the deceased, share a meal, and light candles in their memory. The meal typically includes bread and salt, which symbolizes hospitality and protection. In some cultures, people may include a portion of the meal that the deceased enjoyed as a way to honor them.

Additionally, people will often share stories and memories of the deceased, allowing others to remember and honor their lives. This can be a very powerful and meaningful experience for those in mourning. Candles are lit in the deceased's honor, with each candle representing a different aspect of their life. This can include their spirit, their courage, their joy, or any other qualities that were special to them. After the candles are lit, the Deipnon ritual ends with a few moments of silence to reflect on and remember the person who has passed.

The Deipnon is also observed in a number of different ways. Some people may gather in a physical space to eat and offer prayers, while others may do so in their own homes or even online. Whatever the case, the intention is to honor and pay tribute to the gods and goddesses. It's also important to note that the Deipnon is not limited to any one religion or culture. People from many different religions and cultures observe the Deipnon in their own way, adapting it to their own practices.

Noumenia (New Moon) Ritual

Unlike the Deipnon, which was celebrated on the last day of the month, the Noumenia ritual was celebrated with great enthusiasm on the first day of the new month. It was intended to bring the participants good luck, protection, and prosperity. It was a combination of magical practices and religious observances and was believed to be very powerful.

A powerful form of divination, the Noumenia ritual was based on the movements of the stars and planets. Participants would study the heavens to determine the most auspicious times to perform the ritual. It was believed that the gods were watching the ritual and would intervene to ensure its success.

Historical Practices

The ritual was usually held in a temple, at home in front of shrines, or outside under the glow of the moon, where the priestesses would conduct the ritual with offerings of grain, fruits, and flowers. After the ritual, the participants would enjoy a feast and exchange good wishes and tokens of appreciation. During the ritual, the participants would also make offerings and recite prayers to the gods and goddesses as a sign of their devotion. The ritual was also believed to be able to ward off bad luck and evil spirits. Participants would burn special incense, chant prayers, and make special offerings to the gods to protect them from any harm.

Modern Day Practices

In modern times, this ritual has become a unique way to connect with the divine and observe the cyclical nature of the universe. It is a time of renewal, reflection, and connection with the spiritual realm. The contemporary practice of Noumenia involves setting aside time to connect with the divine, express gratitude, and focus on what one wants to manifest in the upcoming month. It is a time to take stock of the previous month and plan for the upcoming one. It is an opportunity to make a ritual out of the traditional practices of setting intentions, releasing anything that no longer serves you, and cultivating a sense of gratitude for the present moment. Typically, Noumenia is observed by creating a sacred space, lighting a candle, and connecting with the divine through prayer, meditation, or writing. One can also make offerings to their chosen deity, such as food, incense, or flowers. It is a time to express gratitude for all that has been received and to release any negativity experienced in the previous month.

Home Blessing Ritual

The Hekate Home Blessing Ritual is a great way to bring positive energy and blessings into your home. This ancient ritual uses the power of the goddess Hekate to bring protection and blessings to your home and its inhabitants. The ritual itself is simple and straightforward.

1. Begin by lighting a white candle and placing it in the center of the room.
2. Visualize the white light of the candle radiating throughout the room.
3. As you do so, say a prayer to Hekate (anything you feel is appropriate), asking her to bring her power to your house.
4. Afterward, sprinkle some sea salt around the room, saying, *"May the protection of Hekate surround this room."*
5. Next, light some incense, saying, *"Hekate, bless my home with your protection and blessings."*
6. Allow the incense to burn for a few minutes, and then blow it out.
7. Finally, take some essential oil and anoint yourself, saying, *"Hekate, grant me protection and blessings."* You can also anoint the doorways and windows in your home.

Crossroads (Transition/New Beginnings) Ritual

Difficult times can be a real challenge for many of us, and it's during these moments that Hekate's Crossroads can be a true source of strength and guidance. Hekate is the goddess of the crossroads. She holds the key, the flame, and the wheel, which allows her to provide insight and direction to those who seek it. The key to Hekate's crossroads is unlocking the potential within us. You use this key to unlock your deepest desires and dreams and explore the possibilities. The flame of Hekate's crossroads is the spark of inspiration that helps you to stay focused and motivated during difficult times. You can use this flame for kindling your passion and staying on course. The wheel of Hekate's crossroads serves as a reminder that life is full of cycles and that no matter how hard things may seem right now, they will eventually come to an end.

Historical Practices

The Hekate crossroads ritual is an ancient form of witchcraft that has been around for centuries. It is believed to be a powerful form of magic that can significantly change one's life. This ritual is typically performed at a crossroads, which is considered a place of transition, transformation, and new beginnings. The practice involves the practitioner constructing a makeshift altar at the crossroads, upon which offerings such as coins, food, incense, and candles are placed. After making these offerings, the practitioner invokes Hekate and recites an invocation or prayer. This is then followed by a series of spells or chants meant to bring about the desired result. After the ritual, the practitioner leaves the crossroads, leaving the offerings behind, sometimes buried in the earth, as a thank you to Hekate. This practice was believed to bring luck, success, and protection from any negative energies encountered during the transition or new start. The Hekate crossroads ritual is believed to be incredibly powerful and should be used with caution.

Modern Day Practices

The Hekate crossroads ritual is still practiced today, though it has evolved over time. Some practitioners opt to use modern symbols to honor Hekate, such as a candle or incense, and the ritual can be adapted to fit any personal needs. No matter how or where the ritual is conducted, it is still considered an effective way to honor Hekate and mark a transition to facilitate new beginnings. Modern-day rituals involve standing at whatever you use as your version of a crossroads, usually at midnight, and calling out to the Goddess Hekate three times. Offerings such as food, wine, incense, or coins can be made to help set the intention of the ritual. After the offerings are given, one should meditate and express their desire for a transition to Hekate. Following the meditation, it is important to thank the Goddess for her time and guidance. With the completion of this ritual, one should have the energy and clarity to make the changes necessary for a successful and prosperous change.

Protection (Ghosts/Demon/Psychic Attacks) Ritual

The following Hekate protection ritual is designed to keep negative energies away and bring protection and blessings into your life. You can use it to ward off anything you believe brings bad energy into your life.

Preparation

Before performing a Hekate protection ritual, it is important to prepare for the ritual. This includes cleansing and purifying the altar, gathering the necessary tools and items, and creating a sacred space.

1. Create a sacred space. This can be done by lighting candles, burning incense, and setting up an altar. The altar should be decorated with symbols of Hekate, such as a crescent moon or a triple goddess statue.
2. Cleanse and purify the altar. You can do this by smudging the altar with sage or other herbs or using salt and water to cleanse the area. This removes any negative energies that may be present and creates a peaceful and sacred space.
3. Gather the necessary tools and items. This can include candles, incense, herbs, crystals, and offering bowls. It is also important to create an offering for Hekate, such as a small dish of honey, milk, or any other gift you feel is appropriate.

Hekate Protection Rituals for Protection

The following Hekate protection ritual is designed to keep negative energies away and bring protection and blessings into your life.

1. First, light a white candle and place it on the altar
2. Then, light some incense and place it on the altar as well.
3. As the incense burns, recite the following invocation: *"Hekate, goddess of the night, Protect me from all that is not right. Keep away all evil, harm, and strife, and bring protection to my life."*

    For protection for the home and family, recite the following: *"Hekate, goddess of the night, Protect my home and family from all that is not right. Keep away all evil, harm, and strife, and bring protection and peace into our lives."*
4. Next, sprinkle salt around yourself and the altar to create a circle of protection.
5. Then, sprinkle some dried herbs around the altar, such as rosemary or lavender. As you do this, recite the following: *"Hekate, goddess of the night, Protect me and keep me from all that is not right. Bless me with protection and peace of mind and bring blessings to my life."*
6. Finally, make an offering to Hekate. This could be a small dish of honey or milk, or a few coins or other offerings. As you make the offering, recite the following: *"Hekate, goddess of the night, accept this offering as a sign of my gratitude. I thank you for your protection and blessings and for keeping me safe from all that is*

not right."

For protection trials for the home and family, recite the following: *"Hekate, goddess of the night, Accept this offering as a sign of my gratitude. I thank you for your protection and blessings and for keeping us safe from all that is not right."*

7. After completing the ritual, let the candle and incense burn until they are extinguished.

These rituals are often done in the dark of the night, as this is when the goddess is said to be most powerful.

As the goddess of witchcraft, crossroads, and the underworld, Hekate has been venerated in many forms and ways throughout the ages. Hekate rituals are typically focused on honoring the goddess and her qualities and gaining her favor and protection. Typically, these rituals involve offerings of food, incense, and other items that are sacred to her. These offerings can be placed at crossroads and other locations where she is said to dwell. Additionally, some practitioners perform invocations and spell to honor the goddess, and some even perform animal sacrifices to her. Hekate rituals are often celebrated on the night of the new moon, as this is said to be the time when the goddess is strongest and most powerful. Regardless of the ritual, the main theme is always reverence and respect for the goddess and her tremendous power.

Chapter 8: Hekatean Spellwork

This chapter has spells that include prayers to Hekate, Hekatean herbs, plants, and oils, her symbols, and anything else that might associate with her. You can use these tools to draw on Hekate's power to protect your home, loved and yourself, getting advice in challenging situations or guidance through crossroads.

Hekate Mojo Bag

Creating a Hekate mojo bag is one of the easiest ways to harness the goddess's protective powers and combine them with your own power. Once your pouch is done, you can carry or place it anywhere you want. For example, you can put it in your bag or pocket and bring it wherever you go. Anytime you feel the need for a little protective energy boost, you can take the pouch out, and you'll be reminded of the protection you have. Prepare this bag at night, preferably around the full moon.

Ingredients:
- A small, mesh bag
- A piece of ribbon
- Small items collected from crossroads
- An obsidian
- A moonstone
- Lavender, dandelion, and cardamom (preferably in dried, lose form)
- A purple candle

Instructions:
1. Prepare your altar and tools by cleansing them with your favorite incense. This will also help you clear out your energy.
2. Light the candle, place all the ingredients into the mesh bag, and close it with the ribbon.
3. Keep the pouch in your hands for 10 minutes to imbue it with your energy. While charging the bag, you can reach out to Hekate and ask her to add her power to it. Say this when calling on Hekate:

    "Hekate, you who are on both sides and in between,
    You who reside in the crossroads, who guard the threshold,
    I implore you to protect me.
    Grant me safe passage as I navigate through life.
    Protect me in every new space and from negative spirits
    Protect me forces lurking in the in-between spaces
    Hekate, hear my prayer!"

4. When you feel ready, snuff out the candle and place the pouch where you intend to use it. From time to time, you'll need to recharge it with your energy and that of the goddess to keep its powers.

Hekate Essential Oil Blend

This essential oil blend can be used for several purposes, including protection, spiritual communication, and pathway clearing. You can apply it to candles and other items you want to infuse with the goddess's power or use it in spells when working with Hekate. Prepare the oil blend on the night of the full moon, and let it charge until the dark phase of the moon.

Ingredients:
- Poppy
- Lavender
- Mayapple
- Mugwort
- Dirt for a crossroads
- Garlic

- Hair from a dog (preferably black)
- A bottle
- Olive oil or walnut oil

Instructions:

1. Working under the full moon (outside or near a window), mix all the ingredients (except the oil).
2. Pour the mixture into a bottle, and fill the leftover space with the oil
3. Leave the bottle outside or on the windowsill to soak in the moonlight and the goddess's energy.
4. When it's charged, carry it over to your altar and leave it there until the dark moon. Shake it from time to time to imbue it with your energy.

Home Protection Blend

With this herbal blend, you can invoke Hekate's power as the protector, averter of hostile forces, and the protector of crossroads and thresholds. It uses herbs associated with the goddess and salts that also contribute to the protection of your home. You can sprinkle them near windows and doors or at a threshold shrine that protects your home from the inside out. This will only require you to place the image or symbols of the goddess on a shelf near the entrances. If you opt for this method, leave small offerings as well (even if you can only offer spiritual messages).

Ingredients:

- A sprinkle of poppy powder to confuse malicious spirits
- A sprinkle of garlic powder for protection
- A sprinkle of white sage powder for good luck
- A small handful of dirt from the crossroads or brick dust
- A charcoal disk
- The representation of the goddess
- A purple candle

Instructions:

1. Mix the herbs together in a small bowl. Use a little of their herbs (together with essential oils) for anointing the purple candle. This adds another layer of protection to your home. When doing this,

say the following:

"Hekate, I light this candle in your honor.

Just as its flame burns bright, so may your torches burn and guide me eternally.

I ask you to look upon my home as I am your devoted follower.

Grant me this favor and protect my home from harm and mishap."

2. Pour some of the dried herbal mixtures onto the charcoal disk and burn it while reciting the following prayer:

    "Goddess Hekate, I invoke you as I burn these herbs for you. I ask you to bless them as they are from your sacred garden.

    Lend them your protection and grant me your blessing.

    I implore you to imbue the rest of the herbs with enough resilience to protect my home."

3. Combine the herbs with the dirt or brick powder. Let the purple candle burn down completely, but don't leave it unattended. You can do this throughout several nights during the dark phase of the moon.

4. When the candle has completely melted, gather the wax, and put it in a small pouch. You can use this as a charm by hanging it up near the entrance, next to the small altar on the shelf. Alternatively, you can bury the pouch outside your home on your property.

5. Give offerings to the goddess at your altar. Then, carry the herbs to the altar at the entrance of your home and sprinkle them across the thresholds. Or, disperse them around all the entry points (including all windows and doors). When doing this, address Hekate with the following prayer:

    "Hekate, as I stand before this threshold, I place these herbs before you and ask for your guidance and protection.

    Please protect my home and those living in it.

    May all the negative energies be kept away, and may your power bless this place.

    May my entrances always be protected by you,

> *and may you never cease to shield me from malicious influences.*
>
> *Hekate, avert any misfortune and watch over me as your devoted follower.*
>
> *Grant me this favor so I may have safe shelter."*

6. Now, you'll have a powerful significant barrier protecting your home and those living there.
7. You can repeat the spell regularly as needed, although some recommend doing this once a year. However, occasionally recharging your herbal blend will allow you to keep the protection longer without redoing it.
8. Every time you cross the entrance, say a quick prayer of appreciation to Hekate. If you have a small altar near the main entrance, do it there. With each word of gratitude, you're building your connection to the goddess, and she will be more inclined to help you out.

Keybearer Spell

Using old keys as protective charms, you can draw on Hekate's power to find guidance, and protection, open new paths, or have questions answered. For example, suppose you put a key under your pillow after this keybearer spell. In that case, you can communicate with Hekate in your dreams. You can hang the keys above your altar, place them on top, or wear them on a necklace as a good luck charm. You can also use spells designed to find a lost object or unlock secrets and lock your home in a protective layer.

Ingredients:
- A key
- A small box with a latch
- A black candle
- Other candles associated with your intention
- Rosemary, sage, and lavender in dried, loose form
- Paper and pen
- Incense of your choice

Instructions:
1. Gather your supplies during a waxing or full moon phase - the latter will give you full potency.
2. Purify your space and tools by smudging, placing them in salt, or whatever cleansing method you prefer.
3. Light the candles associated with your purpose and the incense, and turn down any artificial lights.
4. Light the black candle and say:

    "I call on Hekate, the Keybearer, to fill this candle flame with her ancient wisdom and magical essence.

    May it empower my spell for protection."
5. Take a piece of paper, and write down your clear intention (focusing on what you want to protect, unlock, or hide) and the paper several times towards you.
6. Put the paper in the box and sprinkle the herbs over it while asking each to enact their powers. Close the box and visualize how you manifest your intent. For example, if you want to unlock secrets in your dreams, picture yourself lying down on the bed and speaking with Hekate in your dreams.
7. Take your key, and holding it above the candle flame, say:

    "May this key ward off evil and negative influences."

    I bear the key now, and I shall unlock its power."
8. Place the key under your pillow to find answers in your dreams. Go to bed and wait for your answers. When you receive them, write them down as soon as you wake up.
9. You can unlock the box and release the spell when you get your answers.

Strophalos Crystal Grid

Crystal grids are great for concentrating and combining the strengths of the individual stones. Using a Strophalos crystal grid lets you draw on Hekate's power to protect your home. You can set it up near a window and channel its energy outside the house with the goddess's help. It's recommended to do this during the darkest phase of the moon when the moon's liminal power is the strongest. This way, the grid protects your home for all spirits – from this world, the underworld, and those residing in between.

Ingredients:
- A Strophalos (Hekate's Wheel grid mat - you can draw a grid on a piece of cloth on your own or buy one premade)
- Stones associated with Hekate (jade, obsidian, ruby, sapphire, pearl, jasper, moonstone)
- Other stones you feel drawn to
- A large bowl
- Candles

Instructions:
1. Start by cleansing and charging the stones. The most effective way to do this is to place them in a bowl and leave them on a windowsill for at least one night during the waning phase of the moon.
2. Set your intentions by visualizing, journaling, or otherwise bringing your desire into focus. Use present tense and a positive tone. For example, instead of saying: *"I don't want my home to be defenseless,"* say: *"My home is protected."*
3. Clean the place where you want to keep your grid from clutter, and use smudging to banish harmful energies. Slowly carry your smudging stick around your home to make sure that the negative energy is eliminated from every corner.
4. Place the cloth with the grid on the designated space. Focusing on your intention, begin placing the crystals around the pattern. Keep each stone in your hands for a few seconds to infuse them with your energy.
5. If you have trouble concentrating, start by putting the first crystal in the middle to center you and the energy of the crystals. This first crystal should correspond to the fundamental purpose of your grid. For Hekate's protection, place obsidian in the middle. Putting a piece of paper with your intention or a symbol attached to it also helps focus the grid's energy.
6. Place the remaining crystals around the middle one. When you're finished, move on to charging your grid. You can do this by meditating on your intent or through any other means that help you connect with your magical tools.

7. Once your intentions are set, you can dismantle the grid or leave it as it is until you start to see the effects. If you keep it, make sure to revisit it each night and say a prayer to Hekate.

Strophalos Necklace Charm

This necklace charm has one of the ancient symbols associated with the goddess - Hekate's wheel. Also called the symbol of the triple goddess, this tool can be a powerful ally for psychic protection. By charging it, you can empower it with Hekate's energy, while wearing it will ensure that the charms stay in contact with your energy. If you feel that you're being influenced by negative psychic energy, touch your pendant to remind yourself that you have the power to ward off negative influences.

Ingredients:
- A necklace with a pendant depicting Hekate's wheel
- Salt - in a little bowl
- Incense
- 1 Moonstone
- 1 Obsidian
- Jasper
- A black candle
- Representations of the goddess, such as keys, symbols of her animals, or death

Instructions:
1. Place your ingredients on your altar at dusk during the full moon phase. Keep your window open to let the moonlight in.
2. Place the pendant and the necklace into the bowl of salt. You can move the windowsill under the moonlight for a few minutes to charge it with the goddess's power.
3. For the best results, prepare yourself by taking a cleansing bath while your jewelry is cleansed and charged.
4. When you're done with your bath, light the candle and place it in the middle of the altar. Put the representation of the goddess next to the candle.
5. Place the three stones in front of you on the altar in a semicircle. Take out the jewelry from the bowl and place it in front of the stones.

6. Call on Hekate with the following prayer:

   "Hekate, I ask you to hear my prayers!

   I call upon you to protect me from evil spirits.

   Shield me from those who do not rest but roam the world, wanting to cause harm.

   You who rule those spirits less than god, please withdraw them from my presence.

   Hekate, Gate-Keeper of the Crossroads, protect my psyche from negative energies and banish malevolence from my presence!"

7. Take the charm into your hands and feel its warm, protective energy. Place it around your neck, and wear it to remain protected from malevolent spiritual energies.

Hekate's Open Pathway Spell

This spell can invoke Hekate, whether you want to work with her as the Torch Bearer, the Keeper of Keys, or the. You can use it to cleanse your path from negative influences, uncover new opportunities, or find the road to a successful life. The spell incorporates several items associated with Hekate, including herbs and symbols of the animals.

Ingredients:
- Keys and other symbols of Hekate
- 3 orange candles
- Lavender essential oil
- A mixture of sage, cinnamon, lavender, dandelion root, and frankincense
- Dirt from a crossroads
- Incense of your choice (sage is best for cleansing and protection)
- Offerings for Hekate (food, art, or whatever you wish to gift)

Instructions:
1. At night, during the darkest phase of the moon, prepare your tools by placing them on your altar. Start by adorning the space with symbols you use for representing the goddess (minus one key).

2. Light your incense and focus on your intention.
3. Anoint the three candles in lavender essential oil and the herbal mixture. The sacred herbs of Hekate will provide guidance, cleansing, and success in your magical pursuit.
4. Place the candles in the middle of the altar in an inverted triangle. Sprinkle the crossroad dirt and more loose herbs around the candles. When sprinkling the herbs, make a line between each candle.
5. Put a key between the three candles, and make an offering to the goddess. Then start reciting the following prayer while lighting the first candle:

    "Hekate, Guardian of the Crossroads, I seek you.

    I ask you to open my paths and cleanse them of energetic blockages, misfortune,

    and anything that would steer me from my path."
6. Lighting the second candle, chant:

    "Hekate, shine your bright lights upon my path to prosperity.

    Torch Bearer, steer me away from misguided paths.

    May your flames burn eternal and illuminate my road to success."
7. Lighting the third candle, say:

    "Keeper of the Keys, open the doors to a journey that leads to new opportunities and victory.

    Hekate, I ask you to Bless me with luck, good fortune, and the key to triumph.

    You who are found in every crossroads, help me avoid closed doors."
8. Take a deep breath, sit back, and continue with your prayer:

    "Hekate, Patron of all Witches, listen to my prayers. As I light these candles, may their flame bestow me power as potent as the fire of your torches.

    Clear my ways on this journey, and show me the way to unlock the best opportunities. Goddess Hekate, I implore you to empower this spell with all your divine essence."

9. Let the candle burn all the way down, but don't leave them unattended. You can relight them as many times as it takes them to burn down. When they're finished, dispose of the wax at a crossroads.
10. Carry the key from the spell as a charm. When you receive the blessing you asked for, make another offering to express your gratitude to Hekate.

Chapter 9: Divination with Hekate

Divination is the practice of predicting the future by interpreting signs, omens, and messages in nature. It is an ancient form of foretelling used throughout history to seek insight into relationships, finances, health, and more. Divination serves as a way for individuals to understand what lies ahead or to receive guidance about their current situation or course of action.

This practice can help you make sense of your life and gain clarity about what may be in store for you in the future. Seeking guidance from divination practices can increase your knowledge and understanding of past events, enabling you to plan for the future with greater insight. By tapping into this guide, you can also gain greater self-awareness and become more attuned to any energies or situations that may be hindering your progress.

Moreover, divination allows you to understand yourself better and reveals your hidden gifts and talents. It also provides access to spiritual knowledge that may not be readily available through other means. Making decisions based on a higher level of understanding than just gut instinct alone allows you to tap into your inner wisdom, which can guide you on how best to respond when faced with challenging situations. Additionally, divinatory practices can guide you toward taking the necessary steps for personal growth, thereby enabling you to reach your goals faster and more effectively.

Using divination can foster a deeper connection between you and the divine, revealing deeper truths about yourself and offering practical daily life advice that promotes physical wellness and emotional balance. Through these readings, you can better understand yourself on a deeper level, leaving room for meaningful change within your life.

Goddess Hekate's Role in Divination

Goddess Hekate has long been associated with divination and prophecy. In ancient Greek mythology, Hekate was often portrayed as a powerful Goddess of supernatural knowledge, linking the mortal world with the divine realms. She was the goddess of the crossroads, and her presence in those places allowed her to be seen as a bringer of messages from the future. She is also associated with dark magic and necromancy, making her an ideal figure for divination rituals.

In many cultures, Hekate is seen as a guardian of doorways between worlds, and this connection to travel makes it easy to see how she became tied to divination. For instance, tarot cards are tools Hekate used to travel through space and time, allowing her to communicate more effectively with mortals in the present day. These cards allow one to access past events or gain information about future events. Additionally, Hekate is often associated with astrology and lunar cycles. Ancient Greeks would consult her prior to embarking on any journey or making major decisions in life as she was believed to offer insight into what was ahead.

Hekate's association with necromancy also ties into divination. Communicating with the dead can provide insights into unknowns in the living world. This could take many forms. One could use mediums or seers who specialized in interpreting signs from beyond, consulting occult texts for advice about life and death, or even engaging in trance-like states where visions from beyond could be revealed. All these methods combined (tarot cards, astrology/lunar cycles & necromancy) allowed Hekate to provide devotees seeking knowledge - both mundane & spiritual - a way to access deeper layers of insight that allowed them to make informed decisions based on a more holistic approach than relying solely on physical evidence alone.

Divination Arts Associated with Hekate
1. Crystal Ball Scrying

Crystal ball scrying is an ancient form of divination that involves looking into an orb-shaped object, such as a crystal ball or reflective surface, to receive insights and messages from the spiritual realm. This practice is believed to be centuries old and has frequently been used by mystics and psychics alike to invoke visions of the future. It can also be used to gain a greater understanding of one's personal life experiences. During crystal ball scrying, the practitioner focuses their gaze deeply into the sphere while breathing deeply in an effort to reach a meditative state. Once these methods have been accomplished, images may appear within the crystal ball that is then interpreted according to the individual's beliefs and knowledge of symbolism. When interpreting these images, practitioners need to remain open-minded and non-judgmental in order for them to gain deeper insight into what they are seeing. In addition to receiving prophetic messages, those who engage with this practice often report feeling peacefulness, clarity of mind, and higher levels of intuition.

Crystal ball scrying can be enhanced with Hekatean magic, as it is rooted in the same spiritual energy of the goddess Hekate.

Hekatean magic can be incorporated into crystal ball scrying by first preparing the space, setting up your altar, and gathering supplies like incense, candles, herbs, stones, or tarot cards corresponding to the goddess's energies. An altar with images of Hekate should also be present, along with other items that represent her domains, such as keys, coins, and herbs. Candles in shades of purple, black, silver, or white should be lit around the area as symbols of Hekate's presence. Incense of myrrh or frankincense can also be used to increase the energies surrounding the ritual space. Then, you should offer a prayer or invocation to invoke her spirit into the room and allow her energy to infuse your practice.

When ready, an invocation of Hekate should be spoken or sung aloud to call upon her guidance and power. This invocation should express gratitude for her presence and ask for protection from dangers that may arise during the scrying session. Once this invocation is complete, one can move on to gazing into their crystal ball to receive messages from spirit realms beyond our own.

Once the space is prepared and blessed, it's time to begin scrying with the crystal ball. Begin by holding the ball in both hands while focusing on Hekate's energy and asking for guidance. Asking questions silently within yourself will bring forth psychic visions from within the depths of the crystal ball. Focus your vision on the depths of the sphere as if looking through a window into another realm, allowing images and symbols to appear before your inner eye to provide insight into the question asked.

The energies that flow through the crystal ball can be used to help interpret these visions. For example, if you see symbols related to protection or guardianship during scrying, you may want to consider how this ties into Hekate's protective energy and reflect on what it means for your life. While looking into the crystal ball, it is important to remain open and relaxed to best receive information from these unseen realms through visual images or thoughts that come up from within oneself or from outside sources. Additionally, using tarot cards with the same themes as Hekate's realm - like death and rebirth, crossing boundaries, or navigating darkness - can further enhance your divination practice by providing a more in-depth interpretation of the messages from the crystal ball.

When your scrying session has ended, thank Hekate for her guidance before releasing her energy from the room. You can use another prayer or invocation, and the ritual should end with extinguishing any candles or incense that have been used.

Combining crystal ball scrying with Hekatean magic makes it possible to reach a deeper understanding of one's life path and gain insight into the mysteries of the world around you. As an ancient goddess who has long been associated with portals between realms, Hekate's energies are invaluable when exploring the unknown through divination. By inviting her spirit into your practice, you will be able to access powerful guidance from beyond our physical realm and make use of her magic in a safe and informed way.

By incorporating Hekate into crystal ball scrying, great insights can be obtained by connecting with her immense energy. She will use her dominion over magic and mysticism to assist you properly when you call upon her. When done properly, crystal ball scrying is a powerful practice that can allow for exploration beyond the physical realm. Hekate will guide you on your path if you are willing to reach out for her help.

2. Black Mirror Scrying

Black mirror scrying is an ancient divinatory psychic practice whereby one peers into a surface, usually a black or dark-colored mirror, for insight, reflection, and connection. It has been used since antiquity to connect with the spiritual world and reveal hidden knowledge. The only real tools needed are a still and dark room, a black mirror made of obsidian or hematite, or an empty bowl or container filled with still water. This process encourages enhanced intuition and allows a person to probe deeper into their subconscious mind to gain insight into situations or better understand oneself.

When practicing black mirror scrying, Hekate's presence can be invoked to aid in connecting with the spirit world and gaining insight from beyond the veil of death. To effectively use this magic, it's important to understand the relationship between you and Hekate. She can serve as both a guide and protector, offering her wisdom when called upon for assistance. However, showing respect and avoiding demanding or disrespectful requests is crucial, as Hekate will only respond in kind.

To incorporate Hecatean magic into your black mirror scrying, the first step is to create an altar or sacred space for your ritual work. This space should include items representing the goddess and her power, such as a statue or figurine, candles, incense, and other meaningful objects. Meditating on these objects can help you establish a connection with Hekate and open yourself up to her influence. It's also important to use protective energy when invoking the goddess, such as by drawing a circle around yourself with salt to create a boundary between you and any negative entities present during the ritual.

In addition to setting up a sacred space, you can use symbols associated with Hekate during the black mirror scrying ritual. For example, a triskele, a three-legged wheel, can represent knowledge gained through journeys between worlds, symbolizing the process of crossing over into non-physical realms via black mirror scrying. You can draw a representation of the triskele on the surface of the black mirror or place it nearby during the ritual. Additionally, you can incorporate various plants associated with Hekate, such as mugwort and mandrake root, known for their ability to bring forth prophetic visions during divinatory practices. Adding these plants either directly onto the surface of the black mirror or placing them near it can enhance its power when used within this type of ceremonial work dedicated to Hekate's patronage.

Besides using visual symbols associated with Hekate, verbal invocations could also be used during a black mirror scrying ritual while asking for guidance from beyond this realm. These should include requests for personal insight and protection while engaging in divination activities such as those involving mirrors. Invocations could take many forms, including spoken word prayers and poem recitations, allowing participants to shape their personal connection with Hekate according to their needs and intentions for that particular session.

Once you have created your altar and established a connection with Hekate, you are ready to begin scrying with the black mirror. Focus your attention on the dark surface of the mirror and allow yourself to go into a meditative state. While visualizing Hekate in her three-headed form, ask her for assistance and guidance to understand what lies beyond the mirror's surface. At this point, many practitioners like to perform a guided visualization exercise or explore their own minds in an effort to uncover hidden knowledge or visions that may appear in the reflection of the black mirror. As you look into its depths, take note of any images, symbols, or words that come to mind, as this can provide valuable insight into your spiritual understanding and personal growth.

Once you feel you have explored your inner thoughts and any visions that may appear in the mirror, thank Hekate for her help before ending the ritual.

Hekatean magic and black mirror scrying can be an incredibly powerful combination when practiced responsibly and with respect for the goddess' power. With their combined forces, one can uncover inner truths and gain insight into what lies ahead, allowing them to make choices based on knowledge rather than fear or uncertainty.

By incorporating Hekatean magic in black mirror scrying, one can open themselves up to a new realm of spiritual exploration and gain insight into their past life, current situation, and future possibilities. When used correctly, this powerful magic can reveal hidden truths about oneself and help guide them on their journey toward personal growth and enlightenment. With practice and dedication, anyone can use these ancient techniques to explore their own power and deepen their connection with the divine.

3. Tarot/Oracle Cards

If you're interested in divination, you may have heard of oracle and tarot cards as popular tools for gaining insight and guidance. Tarot cards, consisting of 78 cards, often incorporate astrological symbols, archetypes, and numerology. The interpretation of these cards relies on the reader's intuition and the symbolism developed over the centuries. On the other hand, oracle cards are simpler in design and usually have 25-40 individual cards that can be used alone or combined with other decks, and the reader's intuition also interprets the meanings. People around the world have used these tools for centuries to access higher wisdom and gain insight into various issues.

If you practice Hekatean magic and are interested in using tarot or oracle cards, you can incorporate Hekate's energy into your readings. For instance, you could use imagery depicting Hekate, such as her classical Greco-Roman form with three heads, on the face of the cards. Alternatively, you could use symbols associated with Hekate, such as keys, torches, snakes, or dogs, to evoke her presence within the deck. With an offering of prayer or ritualistic elements, you can connect with her energy to gain clarity on the issues you're facing.

Additionally, you could incorporate themes closely linked to Hekate's energy, such as cycles. The major arcana cards could represent the cycles of life, death, and rebirth with which Hekate has traditionally been associated. Imagery, such as a snake eating its own tail, or symbols, such as a wheel or spiral, could be used to convey these themes in the readings. Many practitioners of Hekatean witchcraft view tarot cards as vessels that may be used to invoke spiritual guidance from the patron Goddess herself.

Using tarot or oracle cards in combination with Hekatean magic can be a powerful tool for gaining insight and guidance in your spiritual practice. By incorporating Hekate's energy and themes into your readings, you can deepen your connection to her and better understand the issues you're facing.

Hekate also has a strong connection to the moon - especially the new/dark/waning moons - so incorporating this element into Oracle cards would effectively invoke her presence. The card images themselves could involve depictions of crescent moons, stars, wolves howling at the moon, and other symbolic items associated with the lunar cycle. Similarly, Hekate's connection to crossroads and liminal spaces could be explored within Tarot readings using visual motifs such as two roads meeting in the middle of nowhere or a character standing at the edge of a cliff.

In addition to visual elements, her presence could also be invoked through words and phrases - either printed on the cards or used during readings. For example, keywords associated with Hekate, such as "liminal," "cycle," "pathway," or "journey," can invoke her energy. Similarly, affirmations such as "I am present at this moment" could also be included on the face of Oracle cards as a way to remind readers that they are not alone in their journey and that Hekate is there to offer guidance.

Hekatean magic can be incorporated into the structure of Tarot/Oracle readings themselves. Generally speaking, most decks incorporate three-card spreads - each card representing a past, present, and future element. This could be expanded upon to represent the three faces of Hekate in reading. For example, one card could represent her Maiden aspect (past), another card could represent her Mother aspect (present), and the third card could represent her Crone aspect (future). Alternatively, a nine-card spread can also be used to represent Hekate's role as a triple Goddess. In this case, each set of three cards is assigned its own theme or focus area; for example, one set could focus on healing while another set could focus on transformation.

Incorporating Hekatean magic into Tarot/Oracle decks can be a great way to enhance the reading experience and invoke her energy in everyday life. Through visual motifs, words/phrases, and unique spread structures, readers can access Hekate's wisdom interactively and creatively that is still rooted in traditional witchcraft practices.

4. Bone Casting

Hekatean magic can be incorporated into bone casting, also known as scapulimancy. Bone casting divination involves taking a set of animal bones and creating a cast from them to look for patterns that offer insight into the future or answers to questions asked by the ritual participant. Hekate can be invoked in this ritual in several ways. Hekatean bone casting is a specific type of bone divination in which the practitioner uses talismans associated with Hekate, such as crayfish claws, vulture feathers, and mandrake root, to cast bones to glimpse what lies ahead.

Before beginning any magical work, having a proper mindset and focusing your intentions on what you want to gain from experience is important. For Hekatean bone casting, light a candle or incense dedicated to Hekate and say an invocation or prayer asking for her assistance in your divination. During the bone-casting divination ritual, incense offerings are often made to honor Hekate and invite her protection while engaging with spiritual forces. The type of incense used is usually based around herbs sacred to Hekate, such as juniper or cypress, which are believed to bring her closer. Many practitioners will draw a pentacle on the ground before beginning the ritual, invoking Hekate's presence in it. Alternatively, an icon or statue of Hekate can be placed nearby as an offering and symbol of her presence.

After establishing this connection with the goddess, pick out a set of bones you feel drawn to. The type of bone used will vary depending on the practitioner. Once you have picked out your preferred set of bones, cleanse them in a mixture of rosemary and sea salt water before drying them off and charging them with energy through meditation.

Once the bones are charged and ready to be used, it is time to begin casting them. Start by spreading a white cloth on the floor with your chosen set of bones placed in the center. Place both of your hands over the bones, focusing your intentions on what you want to learn from them. Begin slowly rolling the bones around while asking a specific question or focusing on an area of life you want insight into. As you roll the bones, pay close attention to how they interact with each other and if any patterns emerge between them as they move across the cloth. Each bone will have its own significance, so take note of which ones are being rolled together more than others and use intuition to make interpretations.

After completing the bone cast and looking for any patterns that may appear within it, practitioners can choose to ask for further guidance from Hekate by meditating on her iconography or drawing additional symbols connected to her, such as stars or keys. Additionally, you can offer prayers to ask for guidance from her on how best to interpret what was received through the bone-casting reading.

Once you know what the bones might be telling you, take some time to reflect on their messages and consider how they could relate to your current situation or future path. Finally, after receiving any insights gained through this process, it is customary to thank Hekate for her assistance and make offerings once more in gratitude, either verbally or with further incense burning.

Hekatean bone casting is a powerful divination practice that can provide practitioners with valuable insights into both their present and future. By connecting with the goddess Hekate and using intuition while interpreting the messages of the bones, practitioners can better understand their lives and make informed decisions based on the information they receive.

Bonus: Orphic Hymn to Hekate

Translated Text:
"I call Hekate of the Crossroads, worshipped at the meeting of three paths, oh lovely one.

In the sky, earth, and sea, you are venerated in your saffron-colored robes.

Funereal Daimôn, celebrating among the souls of those who have passed.

Persian, fond of deserted places, you delight in deer.

Goddess of night, protectress of dogs, invincible Queen.

Drawn by a yoke of bulls, you are the queen who holds the keys to all the Kózmos.

Commander, Nýmphi, nurturer of children, you who haunt the mountains.

Pray, Maiden, attend our hallowed rituals;

Be forever gracious to your mystic herdsman and rejoice in our gifts of incense."

Original Greek Text:
"Εἰνοδίην Ἑκάτην κλήιζω, τριοδῖτιν, ἐραννήν,

οὐρανίην, χθονίαν τε, καὶ εἰναλίην κρυκόπεπλον,

τυμβιδίην, ψυχαῖς νεκύων μέτα βακχεύουσαν,

Πέρσειαν, φιλέρημον, ἀγαλλομένην ἐλάφοισιν,

νυκτερίην, σκυλακῖτιν, ἀμαιμάκετον βασίλειαν,
ταυροπόλον, παντὸς κόσμου κληιδοῦχον ἄνασσαν,
ἡγεμόνην, νύμφην, κουροτρόφον, οὐρεσιφοῖτιν,
λισσόμενοις κούρην τελεταῖς ὁσίαισι παρεῖναι
βουκόλῳ εὐμενέουσαν ἀεὶ κεχαρηότι θυμῷ."

Conclusion

The goddess Hekate is known for having both good and evil sides. She is the deity of witchcraft, doorways, magic, the moon, necromancy, and creatures associated with nighttime. Hekate's immense power is undeniable, which is why some people associate her with dark power and evil. That said, most people regard her as the deity of protection and guidance. She is often depicted as a beautiful woman holding a torch, signifying her association with darkness and the night. She is also usually depicted with three faces, symbolizing her role as the deity of crossroads and her ability to look and watch over all directions.

Even though she is a widely popular figure in Greek mythology and in the world of witchcraft, she was never initially a member of the Greek pantheon. Like the deities Dionysus and Demeter, Hekate originated in ancient Thrace, which predates ancient Greece. Originally, the goddess was believed to rule over the seas, heavens, and Earth. All deities, including Zeus, the king of the Greek gods, honored Hekate. She was also the only deity at the time to retain her powers after siding with the Olympians to defeat the Titans.

Over time, Hekate's power became more defined, shaping her as the protector goddess of witches, magic, and crossroads we know today. Neopagans regard her as a prominent symbol of their practices and an archetype among the deities. Wiccans, to this day, worship her as the goddess of magic, darkness, and the moon.

Now that you have read this book, you know everything you need to know about Hekate. Learning about her history, stories, how she manifests herself, and what she means to different people can help you work with her more effectively. Knowing all the symbols and tools associated with the goddess will allow you to build the perfect altar and give you ideas about which items to incorporate into your daily life. Making aspects of Hekate a constant part of your life can help you strengthen your relationship with her.

Learning which offerings to give Hekate shows her how much you respect and appreciate her. Giving the deities meaningful offerings is key to building relationships with them. Not all deities prefer the same offerings- what is significant for one deity might be disrespectful to another. This is why you should check which offerings are appropriate to give Hekate once you set up her altar.

After reading this ultimate guide to understanding Hekate, you should've gained insight into how you relate to Hekate and determined the best way to go about your practice. Now that you're ready to start working with the goddess, you can always return to this book for guidance. While you might need the guidance of an experienced practitioner if you want to delve deeper, this book can help you grasp the basics you need to go further on your journey with Hekate.

Here's another book by Mari Silva that you might like

Your Free Gift
(only available for a limited time)

Thanks for getting this book! If you want to learn more about various spirituality topics, then join Mari Silva's community and get a free guided meditation MP3 for awakening your third eye. This guided meditation mp3 is designed to open and strengthen ones third eye so you can experience a higher state of consciousness. Simply visit the link below the image to get started.

https://spiritualityspot.com/meditation

References

(N.d.). Poddtoppen.Se. https://poddtoppen.se/podcast/1481017209/keeping-her-keys/how-to-create-an-altar-of-hekate

(N.d.-a). Pdfgoes.com. https://pdfgoes.com/download/4015389-Hekate%20Liminal%20Rites%20A%20Study%20Of%20The%20Rituals%20Magic%20And%20Symbols%20Of%20The%20Torch%20Bearing%20Triple%20Goddess%20Of%20The%20Crossroads.pdf

(N.d.-b). Pdfgoes.com. https://pdfgoes.com/download/3533918-The%20Temple%20Of%20Hekate%20Exploring%20The%20Goddess%20Hekate%20Through%20Ritual%20Meditation%20And%20Divination.pdf

"HECATE (Hekate) - Greek Goddess of Witchcraft, Magic & Ghosts." n.d. Theoi.com. https://www.theoi.com/Khthonios/Hekate.html.

"Hekate's Deipnon." n.d. Hellenion.org. https://www.hellenion.org/festivals/hekates-deipnon/.

"Honor the Queen of the Night, Hecate on Her Day." n.d. Campaign-archive.com. https://us20.campaign-archive.com/?u=08b2468195beb1c529a55ee1f&id=ad908f9c6a.

"Noumenia." n.d. Hellenion.org. https://www.hellenion.org/festivals/noumenia/.

ASTERIA. (n.d.). Theoi.com. https://www.theoi.com/Titan/TitanisAsteria.html

Bel, Bekah Evie. 2016. "Observing Hekates Deipnon." Hearth Witch Down Under. June 13, 2016. https://www.patheos.com/blogs/hearthwitchdownunder/2016/06/observing-hekates-deipnon.html.

Brannen, Cyndi. 2020. "Leaning into Hekate's Crossroads during Difficult Times." Keeping Her Keys. May 20, 2020.

https://www.patheos.com/blogs/keepingherkeys/2020/05/hekates-crossroads/.

BUST Magazine. (2020, August 26). Let the ancient spirit of Hekate awaken your inner dark goddess. Bust.com. https://bust.com/living/197579-hekate-dark-goddess-spirit-witch-empower.html

Cartwright, M. (2017). Hecate. World History Encyclopedia. http://worldhistory.org/Hecate/

Cartwright, M. (2017). Hecate. World History Encyclopedia. https://www.worldhistory.org/Hecate/

Cosette. 2021. "Observing the Deipnon and Noumenia, Hecate's Monthly Rituals." Divine Hours Priestess | Tarot Reader (blog). Cosette. October 21, 2021. https://cosettepaneque.com/observing-the-deipnon-and-noumenia-hecates-monthly-rituals/.

Creating an altar – the covenant of hekate (CoH). (n.d.). Hekatecovenant.com. http://hekatecovenant.com/rite-of-her-sacred-fires/useful-info/creating-an-altar/

d'Este, S. (2020, August 24). Hekate's wheel & the iynx wheel. Adamantine Muse. https://www.patheos.com/blogs/adamantinemuse/2020/08/hekates-wheel-the-iynx-wheel/

Dharni, A. (2020, August 12). Queen Of The Night flowers blooming in A time-lapse video is nature at its best. India Times. https://www.indiatimes.com/trending/environment/queen-of-the-night-flowers-blooming-time-lapse-video-520110.html

Erickson, J. (2019, June 6). Herbs of Hecate. Medium. https://janerickson.medium.com/herbs-of-hecate-8399d08ca8c6

Fields, K. (2020, January 21). Hecate: 15 ways to work with the goddess of witchcraft. Otherworldly Oracle; FIELDS CREATIVE CONSULTING. https://otherworldlyoracle.com/hecate-goddess/

Fields, K. (2020, January 5). Key Magic, Myth, and a Lock & Key Spell for Protection. Otherworldly Oracle. https://otherworldlyoracle.com/key-magic/

Greek Olympians. (n.d.). Mythopedia. https://mythopedia.com/topics/greek-olympians

Greenberg, M. (2021, March 22). Hecate Greek goddess of witchcraft: A complete guide (2022). MythologySource; Mike Greenberg, PhD. https://mythologysource.com/hecate-greek-goddess/

HECATE (hekate) - Greek goddess of witchcraft, magic & ghosts. (n.d.). Theoi.com. https://www.theoi.com/Khthonios/Hekate.html

Hecate. (n.d.). Hellenicaworld.com. https://www.hellenicaworld.com/Greece/Mythology/en/Hecate.html

Hecate. (n.d.). Mythopedia. https://mythopedia.com/topics/hecate

Hecate: Triple-bodied Greek goddess of witchcraft and keeper of keys. (2022, October 6). Ancient Origins. https://www.ancient-origins.net/myths-legends-europe/hecate-0010707

Hecate's wheel, strophalos meaning, symbolism, origin and uses. (2021, September 29). Symbols and Meanings - Your Ultimate Guide for Symbolism. https://symbolsandmeanings.net/hecates-wheel-strophalos-meaning-symbolism-origin-uses/

Hekate's Open Pathway Spell. (n.d.). Tumblr. https://hekateanwitchcraft.tumblr.com/post/625740934293913600/this-spell-is-similar-to-a-road-opening-spell-but

Hekatean Home Protection. (n.d.). Tumblr. https://hekateanwitchcraft.tumblr.com/post/631719732022771712/hekatean-home-protection

hekateanwitchcraft. (n.d.). Tumblr. https://hekateanwitchcraft.tumblr.com/post/139478162262/hi-i-thought-your-posts-about-your-epithet-for

Huanaco, F. (2021, June 8). Hecate: Goddess symbols, correspondences, myth & offerings. Spells8. https://spells8.com/lessons/hecate-goddess-symbols/

Jason. (n.d.). Mythopedia. https://mythopedia.com/topics/jason

Kabir, S. R. (2022, September 27). Hecate: The goddess of witchcraft in Greek mythology. History Cooperative; The History Cooperative. https://historycooperative.org/hecate-goddess-of-witchcraft/

Keys, K. H. (n.d.). Hekate: Altars and offerings. Keeping Her Keys. https://keepingherkeys.com/blog/f/creating-altars-and-shrines

Keys, K. H. (n.d.). Hekate: The Keeper of keys. Keeping Her Keys. https://keepingherkeys.com/blog/f/hekate-the-keeper-of-keys

Kyteler, E. (n.d.). Herbal offerings for Hecate. Eclecticwitchcraft.com. https://eclecticwitchcraft.com/hecate-herbal-offerings/

Mackay, D. (2021, June 27). Everything you need to know about Hecate (maiden, mother, crone). TheCollector. https://www.thecollector.com/hecate-goddess-magic-witchcraft/

Meeting Hekate at Her Crossroads - Guided Meditation. (n.d.). SoundCloud. https://soundcloud.com/thewitchespath/meeting-hekate-at-her-crossroads-guided-meditation

My Hekate Oil Recipe. (n.d.). Tumblr. https://hekateanwitchcraft.tumblr.com/post/627289683874988032/my-hekate-oil-recipe

Nightly Prayer to Hekate. (n.d.). Tumblr. https://hekateanwitchcraft.tumblr.com/post/136232812112/nightly-prayer-to-hekate

PHOEBE (phoibe) - Greek Titan goddess of the Delphi oracle. (n.d.). Theoi.com. https://www.theoi.com/Titan/TitanisPhoibe.html

Prayer of Devotion for Hekate. (n.d.). Tumblr. https://hekateanwitchcraft.tumblr.com/post/158919116652/prayer-of-devotion-for-hekate

Rhys, D. (2020a, August 20). Hecate's Wheel symbol - origins and meaning. Symbol Sage. https://symbolsage.com/hecate-wheel-symbolism-and-meaning/

Rhys, D. (2020b, September 9). Hecate - Greek goddess of magic and spells. Symbol Sage. https://symbolsage.com/greek-goddess-of-magic/

Signs from Hekate. (n.d.). Tumblr. https://hekateanwitchcraft.tumblr.com/post/629191173466112000/signs-from-hekate

Small Ways to Incorporate Hekate Worship/Devotion into Your Everyday Life. (n.d.). Tumblr. https://hekateanwitchcraft.tumblr.com/post/630069166650356736/small-ways-to-incorporate-hekate-worshipdevotion

Starting with Hekate. (n.d.). Tumblr. https://hekateanwitchcraft.tumblr.com/post/141027130657/starting-with-hekate

Tarotpugs, /. (2017, October 28). Hekate tarot spread. TarotPugs. https://tarotpugs.com/2017/10/28/hekate-tarot-spread/

The Editors of Encyclopedia Britannica. (2023). Hecate. In Encyclopedia Britannica.

The Eldrum Tree. (2016, January 20). Hecate's herbs - part one. Eldrum.co.uk. https://eldrum.co.uk/2016/01/20/hecates-herbs-part-one/

The orphic hymn to Hecate Ækáti. (n.d.). HellenicGods.org. https://www.hellenicgods.org/the-orphic-hymn-to-hecate-aekati---hekate

Thompson, E. (2019, April 30). How to Make a Crystal Grid, a Step-by-Step Guide. Almanac Supply Co. https://almanacsupplyco.com/blogs/articles/how-to-make-a-crystal-grid

Turnbull, L. (2022, October 27). Hecate: Greek goddess of The Crossroads. Goddess Gift; The Goddess Path. https://goddessgift.com/goddesses/hecate/

Uk, C. L. [@charmedlifeuk3341]. (2021, February 6). Hecate meditation-guided journey to goddess Hecate's cave to receive her guidance.

Caro, T. (2021, July 31). Creating a powerful Altar for Hecate (a quick DIY guide). Magickal Spot. https://magickalspot.com/altar-for-hecate/

Welch, M. (2021, August 29). Kidnapped! The shocking story of Persephone and Hades. Definitelygreece.Gr; Rania Kalogirou. https://www.definitelygreece.com/the-story-of-persephone-and-hades/

What is Hekatean Witchcraft? (n.d.). Tumblr. https://hekateanwitchcraft.tumblr.com/post/631201126976471040/what-is-hekatean-witchcraft

Willett, J., & Tucson, T. I. (2019, June 22). 5 things to know about the mysterious queen of cacti, the night-blooming cereus. This Is Tucson

www.ingramcontent.com/pod-product-compliance
Lightning Source LLC
Chambersburg PA
CBHW060528140426
43039CB00004B/203